The Task and Other Poems

William Cowper

CONTENTS.

INTRODUCTION.

After the publication of his "Table Talk" and other poems in March, 1782, William Cowper, in his quiet retirement at Olney, under Mrs. Unwin's care, found a new friend in Lady Austen. She was a baronet's widow who had a sister married to a clergyman near Olney, with whom Cowper was slightly acquainted. In the summer of 1781, when his first volume was being printed, Cowper met Lady Austen and her sister in the street at Olney, and persuaded Mrs. Unwin to invite them to tea. Their coming was the beginning of a cordial friendship. Lady Austen, without being less earnest, had a liveliness that satisfied Cowper's sense of fun to an extent that stirred at last some jealousy in Mrs. Unwin. "She had lived much in France," Cowper said, "was very sensible, and had infinite vivacity."

The Vicar of Olney was in difficulties, with his affairs in the hands of trustees. The duties of his office were entirely discharged by a curate, and the vicarage was to let. Lady Austen, in 1782, rented it, to be near her new friends. There was only a wall between the garden of the house occupied by Cowper and Mrs. Unwin and the vicarage garden. A door was made in the wall, and there was a close companionship of three. When Lady Austen did not spend her evenings with Mrs. Unwin and Cowper, Mrs. Unwin and Cowper spent their evenings with Lady Austen. They read, talked, Lady Austen played and sang, and they all called one another by their Christian names, William, Mary (Mrs. Unwin), and Anna (Lady Austen). In a poetical epistle to Lady Austen, written in December, 1781, Cowper closes a reference to the strength of their friendship with the evidence it gave, —

> "That Solomon has wisely spoken, —
> 'A threefold cord is not soon broken. '"

One evening in the summer of 1782, when Cowper was low-spirited, Lady Austen told him in lively fashion the story upon which he founded the ballad of "John Gilpin. " Its original hero is said to have been a Mr. Bayer, who had a draper's shop in London, at the corner of Cheapside. Cowper was so much tickled by it, that he lay awake part of the night rhyming and laughing, and by the next evening the ballad was complete. It was sent to Mrs. Unwin's son, who sent it to the Public Advertiser, where for the next two or three years it lay buried in the "Poets' Corner, " and attracted no particular attention.

In the summer of 1783, when one of the three friends had been reading blank verse aloud to the other two, Lady Austen, from her seat upon the sofa, urged upon Cowper, as she had urged before, that blank verse was to be preferred to the rhymed couplets in which his first book had been written, and that he should write a poem in blank verse. "I will, " he said, "if you will give me a subject. " "Oh, " she answered, "you can write upon anything. Write on this sofa. " He playfully accepted that as "the task" set him, and began his poem called "The Task, " which was finished in the summer of the next year, 1784. But before "The Task" was finished, Mrs. Unwin's jealousy obliged Cowper to give up his new friend—whom he had made a point of calling upon every morning at eleven—and prevent her return to summer quarters in the vicarage.

Two miles from Olney was Weston Underwood with a park, to which its owner gave Cowper the use of a key. In 1782 a younger brother, John Throckmorton, came with his wife to live at Weston, and continued Cowper's privilege. The Throckmortons were Roman Catholics, but in May, 1784, Mr. Unwin was tempted by an invitation to see a balloon ascent from their park. Their kindness as hosts won upon Cowper; they sought and had his more intimate friendship, till in his correspondence he playfully abused the first syllable of their name and called them Mr. and Mrs. Frog.

Cowper's "Task" went to its publisher and printing was begun, when suddenly "John Gilpin, " after a long sleep in the Public Advertiser, rode triumphant through the town. A favourite actor of the day was giving recitations at Freemason's Hall. A man of letters, Richard Sharp, who had read and liked "John Gilpin, " pointed out to the actor how well it would suit his purpose. The actor was John Henderson, whose Hamlet, Shylock, Richard III., and Falstaff were the most popular of his day. He died suddenly in 1785, at the age of thirty-eight, and it was thus in the last year of his life that his power of recitation drew "John Gilpin" from obscurity and made it the nine days' wonder of the town. Pictures of John Gilpin abounded in all forms. He figured on pocket-handkerchiefs. When the publisher asked for a few more pages to his volume of "The Task, " Cowper gave him as makeweights an "Epistle to Joseph Hill, " his "Tirocinium, " and, a little doubtfully, "John Gilpin. " So the book was published in June, 1785; was sought by many because it was by the author of "John Gilpin, " and at once won recognition. The preceding volume had not made Cowper famous. "The Task" at once gave him his place among the poets.

Cowper's "Task" is to this day, except Wordsworth's "Excursion, " the best purely didactic poem in the English language. The "Sofa" stands only as a point of departure: — it suits a gouty limb; but as the poet is not gouty, he is up and off. He is off for a walk with Mrs. Unwin in the country about Olney. He dwells on the rural sights and rural sounds, taking first the inanimate sounds, then the animate. In muddy winter weather he walks alone, finds a solitary cottage, and draws from it comment upon the false sentiment of solitude. He describes the walk to the park at Weston Underwood, the prospect from the hilltop, touches upon his privilege in having a key of the gate, describes the avenues of trees, the wilderness, the grove, and the sound of the thresher's flail then suggests to him that all live by energy, best ease is after toil. He compares the luxury of art with wholesomeness of Nature free to all, that brings health to the sick, joy to the returned seafarer. Spleen vexes votaries of artificial life. True gaiety is for the innocent. So thought flows on, and touches in its course the vital questions of a troubled time. "The Task" appeared four years before the outbreak of the French Revolution, and is in many passages not less significant of rising storms than the "Excursion" is significant of what came with the breaking of the clouds.

H.M.

THE TASK.

BOOK I. THE SOFA.

["The history of the following production is briefly this: —A lady, fond of blank verse, demanded a poem of that kind from the author, and gave him the SOFA for a subject. He obeyed, and having much leisure, connected another subject with it; and, pursuing the train of thought to which his situation and turn of mind led him, brought forth, at length, instead of the trifle which he at first intended, a serious affair—a volume.]

I sing the Sofa. I, who lately sang
Truth, Hope, and Charity, and touched with awe
The solemn chords, and with a trembling hand,
Escaped with pain from that advent'rous flight,
Now seek repose upon a humbler theme:
The theme though humble, yet august and proud
The occasion—for the Fair commands the song.

Time was, when clothing sumptuous or for use,
Save their own painted skins, our sires had none.
As yet black breeches were not; satin smooth,
Or velvet soft, or plush with shaggy pile:
The hardy chief upon the rugged rock
Washed by the sea, or on the gravelly bank
Thrown up by wintry torrents roaring loud,
Fearless of wrong, reposed his weary strength.
Those barbarous ages past, succeeded next
The birthday of invention; weak at first,
Dull in design, and clumsy to perform.
Joint-stools were then created; on three legs
Upborne they stood. Three legs upholding firm
A massy slab, in fashion square or round.
On such a stool immortal Alfred sat,
And swayed the sceptre of his infant realms;
And such in ancient halls and mansions drear
May still be seen, but perforated sore
And drilled in holes the solid oak is found,
By worms voracious eating through and through.

1

At length a generation more refined
Improved the simple plan, made three legs four,
Gave them a twisted form vermicular,
And o'er the seat, with plenteous wadding stuffed,
Induced a splendid cover green and blue,
Yellow and red, of tapestry richly wrought
And woven close, or needlework sublime.
There might ye see the peony spread wide,
The full-blown rose, the shepherd and his lass,
Lapdog and lambkin with black staring eyes,
And parrots with twin cherries in their beak.

Now came the cane from India, smooth and bright
With Nature's varnish; severed into stripes
That interlaced each other, these supplied,
Of texture firm, a lattice-work that braced
The new machine, and it became a chair.
But restless was the chair; the back erect
Distressed the weary loins that felt no ease;
The slippery seat betrayed the sliding part
That pressed it, and the feet hung dangling down,
Anxious in vain to find the distant floor.
These for the rich: the rest, whom fate had placed
In modest mediocrity, content
With base materials, sat on well-tanned hides
Obdurate and unyielding, glassy smooth,
With here and there a tuft of crimson yarn,
Or scarlet crewel in the cushion fixed:
If cushion might be called, what harder seemed
Than the firm oak of which the frame was formed.
No want of timber then was felt or feared
In Albion's happy isle. The lumber stood
Ponderous, and fixed by its own massy weight.
But elbows still were wanting; these, some say,
An alderman of Cripplegate contrived,
And some ascribe the invention to a priest
Burly and big, and studious of his ease.
But rude at first, and not with easy slope
Receding wide, they pressed against the ribs,
And bruised the side, and elevated high
Taught the raised shoulders to invade the ears.
Long time elapsed or e'er our rugged sires
Complained, though incommodiously pent in,

And ill at ease behind. The ladies first
Gan murmur, as became the softer sex.
Ingenious fancy, never better pleased
Than when employed to accommodate the fair,
Heard the sweet moan with pity, and devised
The soft settee; one elbow at each end,
And in the midst an elbow, it received,
United yet divided, twain at once.
So sit two kings of Brentford on one throne;
And so two citizens who take the air,
Close packed and smiling in a chaise and one.
But relaxation of the languid frame
By soft recumbency of outstretched limbs,
Was bliss reserved for happier days; so slow
The growth of what is excellent, so hard
To attain perfection in this nether world.
Thus first necessity invented stools,
Convenience next suggested elbow-chairs,
And luxury the accomplished Sofa last.

The nurse sleeps sweetly, hired to watch the sick,
Whom snoring she disturbs. As sweetly he
Who quits the coach-box at the midnight hour
To sleep within the carriage more secure,
His legs depending at the open door.
Sweet sleep enjoys the curate in his desk,
The tedious rector drawling o'er his head,
And sweet the clerk below; but neither sleep
Of lazy nurse, who snores the sick man dead,
Nor his who quits the box at midnight hour
To slumber in the carriage more secure,
Nor sleep enjoyed by curate in his desk,
Nor yet the dozings of the clerk are sweet,
Compared with the repose the Sofa yields.

Oh, may I live exempted (while I live
Guiltless of pampered appetite obscene)
From pangs arthritic that infest the toe
Of libertine excess. The Sofa suits
The gouty limb, 'tis true; but gouty limb,
Though on a Sofa, may I never feel:
For I have loved the rural walk through lanes
Of grassy swarth, close cropped by nibbling sheep,

And skirted thick with intertexture firm
Of thorny boughs: have loved the rural walk
O'er hills, through valleys, and by river's brink,
E'er since a truant boy I passed my bounds
To enjoy a ramble on the banks of Thames.
And still remember, nor without regret
Of hours that sorrow since has much endeared,
How oft, my slice of pocket store consumed,
Still hungering penniless and far from home,
I fed on scarlet hips and stony haws,
Or blushing crabs, or berries that emboss
The bramble, black as jet, or sloes austere.
Hard fare! but such as boyish appetite
Disdains not, nor the palate undepraved
By culinary arts unsavoury deems.
No Sofa then awaited my return,
No Sofa then I needed. Youth repairs
His wasted spirits quickly, by long toil
Incurring short fatigue; and though our years,
As life declines, speed rapidly away,
And not a year but pilfers as he goes
Some youthful grace that age would gladly keep,
A tooth or auburn lock, and by degrees
Their length and colour from the locks they spare;
The elastic spring of an unwearied foot
That mounts the stile with ease, or leaps the fence,
That play of lungs inhaling and again
Respiring freely the fresh air, that makes
Swift pace or steep ascent no toil to me,
Mine have not pilfered yet; nor yet impaired
My relish of fair prospect; scenes that soothed
Or charmed me young, no longer young, I find
Still soothing and of power to charm me still.
And witness, dear companion of my walks,
Whose arm this twentieth winter I perceive
Fast locked in mine, with pleasure such as love,
Confirmed by long experience of thy worth
And well-tried virtues, could alone inspire—
Witness a joy that thou hast doubled long.
Thou know'st my praise of Nature most sincere,
And that my raptures are not conjured up
To serve occasions of poetic pomp,
But genuine, and art partner of them all.

How oft upon yon eminence, our pace
Has slackened to a pause, and we have borne
The ruffling wind scarce conscious that it blew,
While admiration feeding at the eye,
And still unsated, dwelt upon the scene!
Thence with what pleasure have we just discerned
The distant plough slow-moving, and beside
His labouring team, that swerved not from the track,
The sturdy swain diminished to a boy!
Here Ouse, slow winding through a level plain
Of spacious meads with cattle sprinkled o'er,
Conducts the eye along his sinuous course
Delighted. There, fast rooted in his bank
Stand, never overlooked, our favourite elms
That screen the herdsman's solitary hut;
While far beyond and overthwart the stream
That, as with molten glass, inlays the vale,
The sloping land recedes into the clouds;
Displaying on its varied side the grace
Of hedgerow beauties numberless, square tower,
Tall spire, from which the sound of cheerful bells
Just undulates upon the listening ear;
Groves, heaths, and smoking villages remote.
Scenes must be beautiful which daily viewed
Please daily, and whose novelty survives
Long knowledge and the scrutiny of years:
Praise justly due to those that I describe.

Nor rural sights alone, but rural sounds
Exhilarate the spirit, and restore
The tone of languid Nature. Mighty winds,
That sweep the skirt of some far-spreading wood
Of ancient growth, make music not unlike
The dash of ocean on his winding shore,
And lull the spirit while they fill the mind,
Unnumbered branches waving in the blast,
And all their leaves fast fluttering, all at once.
Nor less composure waits upon the roar
Of distant floods, or on the softer voice
Of neighbouring fountain, or of rills that slip
Through the cleft rock, and, chiming as they fall
Upon loose pebbles, lose themselves at length
In matted grass, that with a livelier green

Betrays the secret of their silent course.
Nature inanimate employs sweet sounds,
But animated Nature sweeter still
To soothe and satisfy the human ear.
Ten thousand warblers cheer the day, and one
The livelong night: nor these alone whose notes
Nice-fingered art must emulate in vain,
But cawing rooks, and kites that swim sublime
In still repeated circles, screaming loud,
The jay, the pie, and even the boding owl
That hails the rising moon, have charms for me.
Sounds inharmonious in themselves and harsh,
Yet heard in scenes where peace for ever reigns,
And only there, please highly for their sake.

Peace to the artist, whose ingenious thought
Devised the weather-house, that useful toy!
Fearless of humid air and gathering rains
Forth steps the man—an emblem of myself!
More delicate his timorous mate retires.
When Winter soaks the fields, and female feet,
Too weak to struggle with tenacious clay,
Or ford the rivulets, are best at home,
The task of new discoveries falls on me.
At such a season and with such a charge
Once went I forth, and found, till then unknown,
A cottage, whither oft we since repair:
'Tis perched upon the green hill-top, but close
Environed with a ring of branching elms
That overhang the thatch, itself unseen
Peeps at the vale below; so thick beset
With foliage of such dark redundant growth,
I called the low-roofed lodge the PEASANT'S NEST.
And hidden as it is, and far remote
From such unpleasing sounds as haunt the ear
In village or in town, the bay of curs
Incessant, clinking hammers, grinding wheels,
And infants clamorous whether pleased or pained,
Oft have I wished the peaceful covert mine.
Here, I have said, at least I should possess
The poet's treasure, silence, and indulge
The dreams of fancy, tranquil and secure.
Vain thought! the dweller in that still retreat

Dearly obtains the refuge it affords.
Its elevated site forbids the wretch
To drink sweet waters of the crystal well;
He dips his bowl into the weedy ditch,
And heavy-laden brings his beverage home,
Far-fetched and little worth: nor seldom waits
Dependent on the baker's punctual call,
To hear his creaking panniers at the door,
Angry and sad and his last crust consumed.
So farewell envy of the PEASANT'S NEST.
If solitude make scant the means of life,
Society for me! Thou seeming sweet,
Be still a pleasing object in my view,
My visit still, but never mine abode.

Not distant far, a length of colonnade
Invites us; monument of ancient taste,
Now scorned, but worthy of a better fate.
Our fathers knew the value of a screen
From sultry suns, and, in their shaded walks
And long-protracted bowers, enjoyed at noon
The gloom and coolness of declining day.
We bear our shades about us; self-deprived
Of other screen, the thin umbrella spread,
And range an Indian waste without a tree.
Thanks to Benevolus—he spares me yet
These chestnuts ranged in corresponding lines,
And, though himself so polished, still reprieves
The obsolete prolixity of shade.

Descending now (but cautious, lest too fast)
A sudden steep, upon a rustic bridge
We pass a gulf, in which the willows dip
Their pendent boughs, stooping as if to drink.
Hence ankle-deep in moss and flowery thyme
We mount again, and feel at every step
Our foot half sunk in hillocks green and soft,
Raised by the mole, the miner of the soil.
He, not unlike the great ones of mankind,
Disfigures earth, and plotting in the dark
Toils much to earn a monumental pile,
That may record the mischiefs he has done.

The summit gained, behold the proud alcove
That crowns it! yet not all its pride secures
The grand retreat from injuries impressed
By rural carvers, who with knives deface
The panels, leaving an obscure rude name
In characters uncouth, and spelt amiss.
So strong the zeal to immortalise himself
Beats in the breast of man, that even a few
Few transient years, won from the abyss abhorred
Of blank oblivion, seem a glorious prize,
And even to a clown. Now roves the eye,
And posted on this speculative height
Exults in its command. The sheepfold here
Pours out its fleecy tenants o'er the glebe.
At first, progressive as a stream, they seek
The middle field; but scattered by degrees,
Each to his choice, soon whiten all the land.
There, from the sunburnt hay-field homeward creeps
The loaded wain; while, lightened of its charge,
The wain that meets it passes swiftly by,
The boorish driver leaning o'er his team,
Vociferous, and impatient of delay.
Nor less attractive is the woodland scene
Diversified with trees of every growth,
Alike yet various. Here the gray smooth trunks
Of ash, or lime, or beech, distinctly shine,
Within the twilight of their distant shades;
There, lost behind a rising ground, the wood
Seems sunk, and shortened to its topmost boughs.
No tree in all the grove but has its charms,
Though each its hue peculiar; paler some,
And of a wannish gray; the willow such,
And poplar that with silver lines his leaf,
And ash far-stretching his umbrageous arm;
Of deeper green the elm; and deeper still,
Lord of the woods, the long-surviving oak.
Some glossy-leaved and shining in the sun,
The maple, and the beech of oily nuts
Prolific, and the lime at dewy eve
Diffusing odours; nor unnoted pass
The sycamore, capricious in attire,
Now green, now tawny, and ere autumn yet
Have changed the woods, in scarlet honours bright.

O'er these, but far beyond (a spacious map
Of hill and valley interposed between),
The Ouse, dividing the well-watered land,
Now glitters in the sun, and now retires,
As bashful, yet impatient to be seen.

Hence the declivity is sharp and short,
And such the re-ascent; between them weeps
A little Naiad her impoverished urn,
All summer long, which winter fills again.
The folded gates would bar my progress now,
But that the lord of this enclosed demesne,
Communicative of the good he owns,
Admits me to a share: the guiltless eye
Commits no wrong, nor wastes what it enjoys.
Refreshing change! where now the blazing sun?
By short transition we have lost his glare,
And stepped at once into a cooler clime.
Ye fallen avenues! once more I mourn
Your fate unmerited, once more rejoice
That yet a remnant of your race survives.
How airy and how light the graceful arch,
Yet awful as the consecrated roof
Re-echoing pious anthems! while beneath,
The chequered earth seems restless as a flood
Brushed by the wind. So sportive is the light
Shot through the boughs, it dances as they dance,
Shadow and sunshine intermingling quick,
And darkening and enlightening, as the leaves
Play wanton, every moment, every spot.

And now, with nerves new-braced and spirits cheered,
We tread the wilderness, whose well-rolled walks,
With curvature of slow and easy sweep—
Deception innocent—give ample space
To narrow bounds. The grove receives us next;
Between the upright shafts of whose tall elms
We may discern the thresher at his task.
Thump after thump resounds the constant flail,
That seems to swing uncertain and yet falls
Full on the destined ear. Wide flies the chaff,
The rustling straw sends up a frequent mist
Of atoms, sparkling in the noonday beam.

Come hither, ye that press your beds of down
And sleep not: see him sweating o'er his bread
Before he eats it. — 'Tis the primal curse,
But softened into mercy; made the pledge
Of cheerful days, and nights without a groan.

By ceaseless action, all that is subsists.
Constant rotation of the unwearied wheel
That Nature rides upon, maintains her health,
Her beauty, her fertility. She dreads
An instant's pause, and lives but while she moves.
Its own revolvency upholds the world.
Winds from all quarters agitate the air,
And fit the limpid element for use,
Else noxious: oceans, rivers, lakes, and streams
All feel the freshening impulse, and are cleansed
By restless undulation: even the oak
Thrives by the rude concussion of the storm:
He seems indeed indignant, and to feel
The impression of the blast with proud disdain,
Frowning as if in his unconscious arm
He held the thunder. But the monarch owes
His firm stability to what he scorns,
More fixed below, the more disturbed above.
The law, by which all creatures else are bound,
Binds man the lord of all. Himself derives
No mean advantage from a kindred cause,
From strenuous toil his hours of sweetest ease.
The sedentary stretch their lazy length
When custom bids, but no refreshment find,
For none they need: the languid eye, the cheek
Deserted of its bloom, the flaccid, shrunk,
And withered muscle, and the vapid soul,
Reproach their owner with that love of rest
To which he forfeits even the rest he loves.
Not such the alert and active. Measure life
By its true worth, the comforts it affords,
And theirs alone seems worthy of the name
Good health, and, its associate in the most,
Good temper; spirits prompt to undertake,
And not soon spent, though in an arduous task;
The powers of fancy and strong thought are theirs;
Even age itself seems privileged in them

With clear exemption from its own defects.
A sparkling eye beneath a wrinkled front
The veteran shows, and gracing a gray beard
With youthful smiles, descends towards the grave
Sprightly, and old almost without decay.

Like a coy maiden, Ease, when courted most,
Farthest retires—an idol, at whose shrine
Who oftenest sacrifice are favoured least.
The love of Nature and the scene she draws
Is Nature's dictate. Strange, there should be found
Who, self-imprisoned in their proud saloons,
Renounce the odours of the open field
For the unscented fictions of the loom;
Who, satisfied with only pencilled scenes,
Prefer to the performance of a God
The inferior wonders of an artist's hand.
Lovely indeed the mimic works of Art,
But Nature's works far lovelier. I admire,
None more admires, the painter's magic skill,
Who shows me that which I shall never see,
Conveys a distant country into mine,
And throws Italian light on English walls.
But imitative strokes can do no more
Than please the eye, sweet Nature every sense.
The air salubrious of her lofty hills,
The cheering fragrance of her dewy vales,
And music of her woods—no works of man
May rival these; these all bespeak a power
Peculiar, and exclusively her own.
Beneath the open sky she spreads the feast;
'Tis free to all—'tis ev'ry day renewed,
Who scorns it, starves deservedly at home.
He does not scorn it, who, imprisoned long
In some unwholesome dungeon, and a prey
To sallow sickness, which the vapours dank
And clammy of his dark abode have bred
Escapes at last to liberty and light;
His cheek recovers soon its healthful hue,
His eye relumines its extinguished fires,
He walks, he leaps, he runs—is winged with joy,
And riots in the sweets of every breeze.
He does not scorn it, who has long endured

A fever's agonies, and fed on drugs.
Nor yet the mariner, his blood inflamed
With acrid salts; his very heart athirst
To gaze at Nature in her green array.
Upon the ship's tall side he stands, possessed
With visions prompted by intense desire;
Fair fields appear below, such as he left
Far distant, such as he would die to find—
He seeks them headlong, and is seen no more.

The spleen is seldom felt where Flora reigns;
The lowering eye, the petulance, the frown,
And sullen sadness that o'ershade, distort,
And mar the face of beauty, when no cause
For such immeasurable woe appears,
These Flora banishes, and gives the fair
Sweet smiles, and bloom less transient than her own.
It is the constant revolution, stale
And tasteless, of the same repeated joys
That palls and satiates, and makes languid life
A pedlar's pack that bows the bearer down.
Health suffers, and the spirits ebb; the heart
Recoils from its own choice—at the full feast
Is famished—finds no music in the song,
No smartness in the jest, and wonders why.
Yet thousands still desire to journey on,
Though halt and weary of the path they tread.
The paralytic, who can hold her cards
But cannot play them, borrows a friend's hand
To deal and shuffle, to divide and sort
Her mingled suits and sequences, and sits
Spectatress both and spectacle, a sad
And silent cipher, while her proxy plays.
Others are dragged into the crowded room
Between supporters; and once seated, sit
Through downright inability to rise,
Till the stout bearers lift the corpse again.
These speak a loud memento. Yet even these
Themselves love life, and cling to it as he,
That overhangs a torrent, to a twig.
They love it, and yet loathe it; fear to die,
Yet scorn the purposes for which they live.
Then wherefore not renounce them? No—the dread,

The slavish dread of solitude, that breeds
Reflection and remorse, the fear of shame,
And their inveterate habits, all forbid.
Whom call we gay? That honour has been long
The boast of mere pretenders to the name.
The innocent are gay—the lark is gay,
That dries his feathers saturate with dew
Beneath the rosy cloud, while yet the beams
Of day-spring overshoot his humble nest.
The peasant too, a witness of his song,
Himself a songster, is as gay as he.
But save me from the gaiety of those
Whose headaches nail them to a noonday bed;
And save me, too, from theirs whose haggard eyes
Flash desperation, and betray their pangs
For property stripped off by cruel chance;
From gaiety that fills the bones with pain,
The mouth with blasphemy, the heart with woe.

The earth was made so various, that the mind
Of desultory man, studious of change,
And pleased with novelty, might be indulged.
Prospects however lovely may be seen
Till half their beauties fade; the weary sight,
Too well acquainted with their smiles, slides off
Fastidious, seeking less familiar scenes.
Then snug enclosures in the sheltered vale,
Where frequent hedges intercept the eye,
Delight us, happy to renounce a while,
Not senseless of its charms, what still we love,
That such short absence may endear it more.
Then forests, or the savage rock may please,
That hides the sea-mew in his hollow clefts
Above the reach of man: his hoary head
Conspicuous many a league, the mariner,
Bound homeward, and in hope already there,
Greets with three cheers exulting. At his waist
A girdle of half-withered shrubs he shows,
And at his feet the baffled billows die.
The common overgrown with fern, and rough
With prickly gorse, that, shapeless and deformed
And dangerous to the touch, has yet its bloom,
And decks itself with ornaments of gold,

Yields no unpleasing ramble; there the turf
Smells fresh, and, rich in odoriferous herbs
And fungous fruits of earth, regales the sense
With luxury of unexpected sweets.

There often wanders one, whom better days
Saw better clad, in cloak of satin trimmed
With lace, and hat with splendid ribbon bound.
A serving-maid was she, and fell in love
With one who left her, went to sea and died.
Her fancy followed him through foaming waves
To distant shores, and she would sit and weep
At what a sailor suffers; fancy too,
Delusive most where warmest wishes are,
Would oft anticipate his glad return,
And dream of transports she was not to know.
She heard the doleful tidings of his death,
And never smiled again. And now she roams
The dreary waste; there spends the livelong day,
And there, unless when charity forbids,
The livelong night. A tattered apron hides,
Worn as a cloak, and hardly hides, a gown
More tattered still; and both but ill conceal
A bosom heaved with never-ceasing sighs.
She begs an idle pin of all she meets,
And hoards them in her sleeve; but needful food,
Though pressed with hunger oft, or comelier clothes,
Though pinched with cold, asks never.—Kate is crazed!

I see a column of slow-rising smoke
O'ertop the lofty wood that skirts the wild.
A vagabond and useless tribe there eat
Their miserable meal. A kettle slung
Between two poles upon a stick transverse,
Receives the morsel; flesh obscene of dog,
Or vermin, or, at best, of cock purloined
From his accustomed perch. Hard-faring race!
They pick their fuel out of every hedge,
Which, kindled with dry leaves, just saves unquenched
The spark of life. The sportive wind blows wide
Their fluttering rags, and shows a tawny skin,
The vellum of the pedigree they claim.
Great skill have they in palmistry, and more

To conjure clean away the gold they touch,
Conveying worthless dross into its place;
Loud when they beg, dumb only when they steal.
Strange! that a creature rational, and cast
In human mould, should brutalise by choice
His nature, and, though capable of arts
By which the world might profit and himself,
Self-banished from society, prefer
Such squalid sloth to honourable toil.
Yet even these, though feigning sickness oft
They swathe the forehead, drag the limping limb,
And vex their flesh with artificial sores,
Can change their whine into a mirthful note
When safe occasion offers, and with dance,
And music of the bladder and the bag,
Beguile their woes, and make the woods resound.
Such health and gaiety of heart enjoy
The houseless rovers of the sylvan world;
And breathing wholesome air, and wandering much,
Need other physic none to heal the effects
Of loathsome diet, penury, and cold.

Blest he, though undistinguished from the crowd
By wealth or dignity, who dwells secure
Where man, by nature fierce, has laid aside
His fierceness, having learnt, though slow to learn
The manners and the arts of civil life.
His wants, indeed, are many; but supply
Is obvious; placed within the easy reach
Of temperate wishes and industrious hands.
Here virtue thrives as in her proper soil;
Not rude and surly, and beset with thorns,
And terrible to sight, as when she springs
(If e'er she spring spontaneous) in remote
And barbarous climes, where violence prevails,
And strength is lord of all; but gentle, kind,
By culture tamed, by liberty refreshed,
And all her fruits by radiant truth matured.
War and the chase engross the savage whole;
War followed for revenge, or to supplant
The envied tenants of some happier spot;
The chase for sustenance, precarious trust!
His hard condition with severe constraint

Binds all his faculties, forbids all growth
Of wisdom, proves a school in which he learns
Sly circumvention, unrelenting hate,
Mean self-attachment, and scarce aught beside.
Thus fare the shivering natives of the north,
And thus the rangers of the western world,
Where it advances far into the deep,
Towards the Antarctic. Even the favoured isles
So lately found, although the constant sun
Cheer all their seasons with a grateful smile,
Can boast but little virtue; and inert
Through plenty, lose in morals what they gain
In manners, victims of luxurious ease.
These therefore I can pity, placed remote
From all that science traces, art invents,
Or inspiration teaches; and enclosed
In boundless oceans, never to be passed
By navigators uninformed as they,
Or ploughed perhaps by British bark again.
But far beyond the rest, and with most cause,
Thee, gentle savage! whom no love of thee
Or thine, but curiosity perhaps,
Or else vain-glory, prompted us to draw
Forth from thy native bowers, to show thee here
With what superior skill we can abuse
The gifts of Providence, and squander life.
The dream is past. And thou hast found again
Thy cocoas and bananas, palms, and yams,
And homestall thatched with leaves. But hast thou found
Their former charms? And, having seen our state,
Our palaces, our ladies, and our pomp
Of equipage, our gardens, and our sports,
And heard our music; are thy simple friends,
Thy simple fare, and all thy plain delights
As dear to thee as once? And have thy joys
Lost nothing by comparison with ours?
Rude as thou art (for we returned thee rude
And ignorant, except of outward show),
I cannot think thee yet so dull of heart
And spiritless, as never to regret
Sweets tasted here, and left as soon as known.
Methinks I see thee straying on the beach,
And asking of the surge that bathes the foot

16

If ever it has washed our distant shore.
I see thee weep, and thine are honest tears,
A patriot's for his country. Thou art sad
At thought of her forlorn and abject state,
From which no power of thine can raise her up.
Thus fancy paints thee, and, though apt to err,
Perhaps errs little when she paints thee thus.
She tells me too that duly every morn
Thou climb'st the mountain-top, with eager eye
Exploring far and wide the watery waste,
For sight of ship from England. Every speck
Seen in the dim horizon turns thee pale
With conflict of contending hopes and fears.
But comes at last the dull and dusky eve,
And sends thee to thy cabin, well prepared
To dream all night of what the day denied.
Alas, expect it not. We found no bait
To tempt us in thy country. Doing good,
Disinterested good, is not our trade.
We travel far, 'tis true, but not for naught;
And must be bribed to compass earth again
By other hopes, and richer fruits than yours.

But though true worth and virtue, in the mild
And genial soil of cultivated life
Thrive most, and may perhaps thrive only there,
Yet not in cities oft. In proud and gay
And gain-devoted cities, thither flow,
As to a common and most noisome sewer,
The dregs and feculence of every land.
In cities, foul example on most minds
Begets its likeness. Rank abundance breeds
In gross and pampered cities sloth and lust,
And wantonness and gluttonous excess.
In cities, vice is hidden with most ease,
Or seen with least reproach; and virtue, taught
By frequent lapse, can hope no triumph there,
Beyond the achievement of successful flight.
I do confess them nurseries of the arts,
In which they flourish most; where, in the beams
Of warm encouragement, and in the eye
Of public note, they reach their perfect size.
Such London is, by taste and wealth proclaimed

17

The fairest capital in all the world,
By riot and incontinence the worst.
There, touched by Reynolds, a dull blank becomes
A lucid mirror, in which nature sees
All her reflected features. Bacon there
Gives more than female beauty to a stone,
And Chatham's eloquence to marble lips.
Nor does the chisel occupy alone
The powers of sculpture, but the style as much;
Each province of her art her equal care.
With nice incision of her guided steel
She ploughs a brazen field, and clothes a soil
So sterile with what charms soe'er she will,
The richest scenery and the loveliest forms.
Where finds philosophy her eagle eye,
With which she gazes at yon burning disk
Undazzled, and detects and counts his spots?
In London. Where her implements exact,
With which she calculates, computes, and scans
All distance, motion, magnitude, and now
Measures an atom, and now girds a world?
In London. Where has commerce such a mart,
So rich, so thronged, so drained, and so supplied,
As London, opulent, enlarged, and still
Increasing London? Babylon of old
Not more the glory of the earth, than she
A more accomplished world's chief glory now.

She has her praise. Now mark a spot or two
That so much beauty would do well to purge;
And show this queen of cities, that so fair
May yet be foul; so witty, yet not wise.
It is not seemly, nor of good report,
That she is slack in discipline; more prompt
To avenge than to prevent the breach of law:
That she is rigid in denouncing death
On petty robbers, and indulges life
And liberty, and ofttimes honour too,
To peculators of the public gold:
That thieves at home must hang; but he, that puts
Into his overgorged and bloated purse
The wealth of Indian provinces, escapes.
Nor is it well, nor can it come to good,

That through profane and infidel contempt
Of holy writ, she has presumed to annul
And abrogate, as roundly as she may,
The total ordinance and will of God;
Advancing fashion to the post of truth,
And centring all authority in modes
And customs of her own, till Sabbath rites
Have dwindled into unrespected forms,
And knees and hassocks are wellnigh divorced.

God made the country, and man made the town.
What wonder, then, that health and virtue, gifts
That can alone make sweet the bitter draught
That life holds out to all, should most abound
And least be threatened in the fields and groves?
Possess ye therefore, ye who, borne about
In chariots and sedans, know no fatigue
But that of idleness, and taste no scenes
But such as art contrives, possess ye still
Your element; there only ye can shine,
There only minds like yours can do no harm.
Our groves were planted to console at noon
The pensive wanderer in their shades. At eve
The moonbeam, sliding softly in between
The sleeping leaves, is all the light they wish,
Birds warbling all the music. We can spare
The splendour of your lamps, they but eclipse
Our softer satellite. Your songs confound
Our more harmonious notes. The thrush departs
Scared, and the offended nightingale is mute.
There is a public mischief in your mirth;
It plagues your country. Folly such as yours,
Graced with a sword, and worthier of a fan,
Has made, which enemies could ne'er have done,
Our arch of empire, steadfast but for you,
A mutilated structure, soon to fall.

BOOK II.

THE TIMEPIECE.

Oh for a lodge in some vast wilderness,
Some boundless contiguity of shade,
Where rumour of oppression and deceit,
Of unsuccessful or successful war,
Might never reach me more! My ear is pained,
My soul is sick with every day's report
Of wrong and outrage with which earth is filled.
There is no flesh in man's obdurate heart,
It does not feel for man. The natural bond
Of brotherhood is severed as the flax
That falls asunder at the touch of fire.
He finds his fellow guilty of a skin
Not coloured like his own, and having power
To enforce the wrong, for such a worthy cause
Dooms and devotes him as his lawful prey.
Lands intersected by a narrow frith
Abhor each other. Mountains interposed
Make enemies of nations, who had else
Like kindred drops been mingled into one.
Thus man devotes his brother, and destroys;
And worse than all, and most to be deplored,
As human nature's broadest, foulest blot,
Chains him, and tasks him, and exacts his sweat
With stripes, that mercy, with a bleeding heart,
Weeps when she sees inflicted on a beast.
Then what is man? And what man, seeing this,
And having human feelings, does not blush
And hang his head, to think himself a man?
I would not have a slave to till my ground,
To carry me, to fan me while I sleep,
And tremble when I wake, for all the wealth
That sinews bought and sold have ever earned.
No: dear as freedom is, and in my heart's
Just estimation prized above all price,
I had much rather be myself the slave
And wear the bonds, than fasten them on him.
We have no slaves at home—then why abroad?
And they themselves, once ferried o'er the wave

That parts us, are emancipate and loosed.
Slaves cannot breathe in England; if their lungs
Receive our air, that moment they are free,
They touch our country and their shackles fall.
That's noble, and bespeaks a nation proud
And jealous of the blessing. Spread it then,
And let it circulate through every vein
Of all your empire; that where Britain's power
Is felt, mankind may feel her mercy too.

Sure there is need of social intercourse,
Benevolence and peace and mutual aid,
Between the nations, in a world that seems
To toll the death-bell to its own decease;
And by the voice of all its elements
To preach the general doom. When were the winds
Let slip with such a warrant to destroy?
When did the waves so haughtily o'erleap
Their ancient barriers, deluging the dry?
Fires from beneath and meteors from above,
Portentous, unexampled, unexplained,
Have kindled beacons in the skies, and the old
And crazy earth has had her shaking fits
More frequent, and foregone her usual rest.
Is it a time to wrangle, when the props
And pillars of our planet seem to fail,
And nature with a dim and sickly eye
To wait the close of all? But grant her end
More distant, and that prophecy demands
A longer respite, unaccomplished yet;
Still they are frowning signals, and bespeak
Displeasure in His breast who smites the earth
Or heals it, makes it languish or rejoice.
And 'tis but seemly, that, where all deserve
And stand exposed by common peccancy
To what no few have felt, there should be peace,
And brethren in calamity should love.

Alas for Sicily, rude fragments now
Lie scattered where the shapely column stood.
Her palaces are dust. In all her streets
The voice of singing and the sprightly chord
Are silent. Revelry and dance and show

Suffer a syncope and solemn pause,
While God performs, upon the trembling stage
Of His own works, His dreadful part alone.
How does the earth receive Him? — With what signs
Of gratulation and delight, her King?
Pours she not all her choicest fruits abroad,
Her sweetest flowers, her aromatic gums,
Disclosing paradise where'er He treads?
She quakes at His approach. Her hollow womb,
Conceiving thunders, through a thousand deeps
And fiery caverns roars beneath His foot.
The hills move lightly and the mountains smoke,
For He has touched them. From the extremest point
Of elevation down into the abyss,
His wrath is busy and His frown is felt.
The rocks fall headlong and the valleys rise,
The rivers die into offensive pools,
And, charged with putrid verdure, breathe a gross
And mortal nuisance into all the air.
What solid was, by transformation strange
Grows fluid, and the fixed and rooted earth
Tormented into billows, heaves and swells,
Or with vortiginous and hideous whirl
Sucks down its prey insatiable. Immense
The tumult and the overthrow, the pangs
And agonies of human and of brute
Multitudes, fugitive on every side,
And fugitive in vain. The sylvan scene
Migrates uplifted, and, with all its soil
Alighting in far-distant fields, finds out
A new possessor, and survives the change.
Ocean has caught the frenzy, and upwrought
To an enormous and o'erbearing height,
Not by a mighty wind, but by that voice
Which winds and waves obey, invades the shore
Resistless. Never such a sudden flood,
Upridged so high, and sent on such a charge,
Possessed an inland scene. Where now the throng
That pressed the beach and hasty to depart
Looked to the sea for safety? They are gone,
Gone with the refluent wave into the deep,
A prince with half his people. Ancient towers,
And roofs embattled high, the gloomy scenes

Where beauty oft and lettered worth consume
Life in the unproductive shades of death,
Fall prone: the pale inhabitants come forth,
And, happy in their unforeseen release
From all the rigours of restraint, enjoy
The terrors of the day that sets them free.
Who then, that has thee, would not hold thee fast,
Freedom! whom they that lose thee so regret,
That even a judgment, making way for thee,
Seems in their eyes a mercy, for thy sake.

Such evil sin hath wrought; and such a flame
Kindled in heaven, that it burns down to earth,
And, in the furious inquest that it makes
On God's behalf, lays waste His fairest works.
The very elements, though each be meant
The minister of man to serve his wants,
Conspire against him. With his breath he draws
A plague into his blood; and cannot use
Life's necessary means, but he must die.
Storms rise to o'erwhelm him: or, if stormy winds
Rise not, the waters of the deep shall rise,
And, needing none assistance of the storm,
Shall roll themselves ashore, and reach him there.
The earth shall shake him out of all his holds,
Or make his house his grave; nor so content,
Shall counterfeit the motions of the flood,
And drown him in her dry and dusty gulfs.
What then—were they the wicked above all,
And we the righteous, whose fast-anchored isle
Moved not, while theirs was rocked like a light skiff,
The sport of every wave? No: none are clear,
And none than we more guilty. But where all
Stand chargeable with guilt, and to the shafts
Of wrath obnoxious, God may choose His mark,
May punish, if He please, the less, to warn
The more malignant. If He spared not them,
Tremble and be amazed at thine escape,
Far guiltier England, lest He spare not thee!

Happy the man who sees a God employed
In all the good and ill that chequer life!
Resolving all events, with their effects

And manifold results, into the will
And arbitration wise of the Supreme.
Did not His eye rule all things, and intend
The least of our concerns (since from the least
The greatest oft originate), could chance
Find place in His dominion, or dispose
One lawless particle to thwart His plan,
Then God might be surprised, and unforeseen
Contingence might alarm Him, and disturb
The smooth and equal course of His affairs.
This truth, philosophy, though eagle-eyed
In nature's tendencies, oft overlooks;
And, having found His instrument, forgets
Or disregards, or, more presumptuous still,
Denies the power that wields it. God proclaims
His hot displeasure against foolish men
That live an Atheist life: involves the heaven
In tempests, quits His grasp upon the winds
And gives them all their fury; bids a plague
Kindle a fiery boil upon the skin,
And putrefy the breath of blooming health.
He calls for Famine, and the meagre fiend
Blows mildew from between his shrivelled lips,
And taints the golden ear. He springs His mines,
And desolates a nation at a blast.
Forth steps the spruce philosopher, and tells
Of homogeneal and discordant springs
And principles; of causes how they work
By necessary laws their sure effects;
Of action and reaction. He has found
The source of the disease that nature feels,
And bids the world take heart and banish fear.
Thou fool! will thy discovery of the cause
Suspend the effect, or heal it? Has not God
Still wrought by means since first He made the world,
And did He not of old employ His means
To drown it? What is His creation less
Than a capacious reservoir of means
Formed for His use, and ready at His will?
Go, dress thine eyes with eye-salve, ask of Him,
Or ask of whomsoever He has taught,
And learn, though late, the genuine cause of all.

England, with all thy faults, I love thee still—
My country! and while yet a nook is left,
Where English minds and manners may be found,
Shall be constrained to love thee. Though thy clime
Be fickle, and thy year most part deformed
With dripping rains, or withered by a frost,
I would not yet exchange thy sullen skies
And fields without a flower, for warmer France
With all her vines; nor for Ausonia's groves
Of golden fruitage, and her myrtle bowers.
To shake thy senate, and from heights sublime
Of patriot eloquence to flash down fire
Upon thy foes, was never meant my task;
But I can feel thy fortune, and partake
Thy joys and sorrows with as true a heart
As any thunderer there. And I can feel
Thy follies too, and with a just disdain
Frown at effeminates, whose very looks
Reflect dishonour on the land I love.
How, in the name of soldiership and sense,
Should England prosper, when such things, as smooth
And tender as a girl, all essenced o'er
With odours, and as profligate as sweet,
Who sell their laurel for a myrtle wreath,
And love when they should fight; when such as these
Presume to lay their hand upon the ark
Of her magnificent and awful cause?
Time was when it was praise and boast enough
In every clime, and travel where we might,
That we were born her children. Praise enough
To fill the ambition of a private man,
That Chatham's language was his mother tongue,
And Wolfe's great name compatriot with his own.
Farewell those honours, and farewell with them
The hope of such hereafter. They have fallen
Each in his field of glory; one in arms,
And one in council;—Wolfe upon the lap
Of smiling victory that moment won,
And Chatham, heart-sick of his country's shame.
They made us many soldiers. Chatham, still
Consulting England's happiness at home,
Secured it by an unforgiving frown
If any wronged her. Wolfe, where'er he fought,

Put so much of his heart into his act,
That his example had a magnet's force,
And all were swift to follow whom all loved.
Those suns are set. Oh, rise some other such!
Or all that we have left is empty talk
Of old achievements, and despair of new.

Now hoist the sail, and let the streamers float
Upon the wanton breezes. Strew the deck
With lavender, and sprinkle liquid sweets,
That no rude savour maritime invade
The nose of nice nobility. Breathe soft,
Ye clarionets, and softer still, ye flutes,
That winds and waters lulled by magic sounds
May bear us smoothly to the Gallic shore.
True, we have lost an empire—let it pass.
True, we may thank the perfidy of France
That picked the jewel out of England's crown,
With all the cunning of an envious shrew.
And let that pass—'twas but a trick of state.
A brave man knows no malice, but at once
Forgets in peace the injuries of war,
And gives his direst foe a friend's embrace.
And shamed as we have been, to the very beard
Braved and defied, and in our own sea proved
Too weak for those decisive blows that once
Insured us mastery there, we yet retain
Some small pre-eminence, we justly boast
At least superior jockeyship, and claim
The honours of the turf as all our own.
Go then, well worthy of the praise ye seek,
And show the shame ye might conceal at home,
In foreign eyes!—be grooms, and win the plate,
Where once your nobler fathers won a crown!—
'Tis generous to communicate your skill
To those that need it. Folly is soon learned,
And, under such preceptors, who can fail?

There is a pleasure in poetic pains
Which only poets know. The shifts and turns,
The expedients and inventions multiform
To which the mind resorts, in chase of terms
Though apt, yet coy, and difficult to win—

To arrest the fleeting images that fill
The mirror of the mind, and hold them fast,
And force them sit, till he has pencilled off
A faithful likeness of the forms he views;
Then to dispose his copies with such art
That each may find its most propitious light,
And shine by situation, hardly less
Than by the labour and the skill it cost,
Are occupations of the poet's mind
So pleasing, and that steal away the thought
With such address from themes of sad import,
That, lost in his own musings, happy man!
He feels the anxieties of life, denied
Their wonted entertainment, all retire.
Such joys has he that sings. But ah! not such,
Or seldom such, the hearers of his song.
Fastidious, or else listless, or perhaps
Aware of nothing arduous in a task
They never undertook, they little note
His dangers or escapes, and haply find
There least amusement where he found the most.
But is amusement all? studious of song
And yet ambitious not to sing in vain,
I would not trifle merely, though the world
Be loudest in their praise who do no more.
Yet what can satire, whether grave or gay?
It may correct a foible, may chastise
The freaks of fashion, regulate the dress,
Retrench a sword-blade, or displace a patch;
But where are its sublimer trophies found?
What vice has it subdued? whose heart reclaimed
By rigour, or whom laughed into reform?
Alas, Leviathan is not so tamed.
Laughed at, he laughs again; and, stricken hard,
Turns to the stroke his adamantine scales,
That fear no discipline of human hands.

The pulpit therefore—and I name it, filled
With solemn awe, that bids me well beware
With what intent I touch that holy thing—
The pulpit, when the satirist has at last,
Strutting and vapouring in an empty school,
Spent all his force, and made no proselyte—

I say the pulpit, in the sober use
Of its legitimate peculiar powers,
Must stand acknowledged, while the world shall stand,
The most important and effectual guard,
Support, and ornament of virtue's cause.
There stands the messenger of truth; there stands
The legate of the skies; his theme divine,
His office sacred, his credentials clear.
By him, the violated Law speaks out
Its thunders, and by him, in strains as sweet
As angels use, the Gospel whispers peace.
He stablishes the strong, restores the weak,
Reclaims the wanderer, binds the broken heart,
And, armed himself in panoply complete
Of heavenly temper, furnishes with arms
Bright as his own, and trains, by every rule
Of holy discipline, to glorious war,
The sacramental host of God's elect.
Are all such teachers? would to heaven all were!
But hark—the Doctor's voice—fast wedged between
Two empirics he stands, and with swollen cheeks
Inspires the news, his trumpet. Keener far
Than all invective is his bold harangue,
While through that public organ of report
He hails the clergy, and, defying shame,
Announces to the world his own and theirs,
He teaches those to read whom schools dismissed,
And colleges, untaught; sells accents, tone,
And emphasis in score, and gives to prayer
The adagio and andante it demands.
He grinds divinity of other days
Down into modern use; transforms old print
To zigzag manuscript, and cheats the eyes
Of gallery critics by a thousand arts.—
Are there who purchase of the Doctor's ware?
Oh name it not in Gath!—it cannot be,
That grave and learned Clerks should need such aid.
He doubtless is in sport, and does but droll,
Assuming thus a rank unknown before,
Grand caterer and dry-nurse of the Church.

I venerate the man whose heart is warm,
Whose hands are pure, whose doctrine and whose life,

Coincident, exhibit lucid proof
That he is honest in the sacred cause.
To such I render more than mere respect,
Whose actions say that they respect themselves.
But, loose in morals, and in manners vain,
In conversation frivolous, in dress
Extreme, at once rapacious and profuse,
Frequent in park with lady at his side,
Ambling and prattling scandal as he goes,
But rare at home, and never at his books
Or with his pen, save when he scrawls a card;
Constant at routs, familiar with a round
Of ladyships, a stranger to the poor;
Ambitions of preferment for its gold,
And well prepared by ignorance and sloth,
By infidelity and love o' the world,
To make God's work a sinecure; a slave
To his own pleasures and his patron's pride.—
From such apostles, O ye mitred heads,
Preserve the Church! and lay not careless hands
On skulls that cannot teach, and will not learn.

Would I describe a preacher, such as Paul,
Were he on earth, would hear, approve, and own,
Paul should himself direct me. I would trace
His master-strokes, and draw from his design.
I would express him simple, grave, sincere;
In doctrine uncorrupt; in language plain,
And plain in manner; decent, solemn, chaste,
And natural in gesture; much impressed
Himself, as conscious of his awful charge,
And anxious mainly that the flock he feeds
May feel it too; affectionate in look
And tender in address, as well becomes
A messenger of grace to guilty men.
Behold the picture!—Is it like?—Like whom?
The things that mount the rostrum with a skip,
And then skip down again; pronounce a text,
Cry—Hem; and reading what they never wrote,
Just fifteen minutes, huddle up their work,
And with a well-bred whisper close the scene.

In man or woman, but far most in man,

And most of all in man that ministers
And serves the altar, in my soul I loathe
All affectation. 'Tis my perfect scorn;
Object of my implacable disgust.
What!—will a man play tricks, will he indulge
A silly fond conceit of his fair form
And just proportion, fashionable mien,
And pretty face, in presence of his God?
Or will he seek to dazzle me with tropes,
As with the diamond on his lily hand,
And play his brilliant parts before my eyes,
When I am hungry for the Bread of Life?
He mocks his Maker, prostitutes and shames
His noble office, and, instead of truth,
Displaying his own beauty, starves his flock!
Therefore, avaunt, all attitude and stare
And start theatric, practised at the glass.
I seek divine simplicity in him
Who handles things divine; and all beside,
Though learned with labour, and though much admired
By curious eyes and judgments ill-informed,
To me is odious as the nasal twang
Heard at conventicle, where worthy men,
Misled by custom, strain celestial themes
Through the prest nostril, spectacle-bestrid.
Some, decent in demeanour while they preach,
That task performed, relapse into themselves,
And having spoken wisely, at the close
Grow wanton, and give proof to every eye—
Whoe'er was edified themselves were not.
Forth comes the pocket mirror. First we stroke
An eyebrow; next compose a straggling lock;
Then with an air, most gracefully performed,
Fall back into our seat; extend an arm,
And lay it at its ease with gentle care,
With handkerchief in hand, depending low:
The better hand, more busy, gives the nose
Its bergamot, or aids the indebted eye
With opera glass to watch the moving scene,
And recognise the slow-retiring fair.
Now this is fulsome, and offends me more
Than in a Churchman slovenly neglect
And rustic coarseness would. A heavenly mind

May be indifferent to her house of clay,
And slight the hovel as beneath her care.
But how a body so fantastic, trim,
And quaint in its deportment and attire,
Can lodge a heavenly mind—demands a doubt.

He that negotiates between God and man,
As God's ambassador, the grand concerns
Of judgment and of mercy, should beware
Of lightness in his speech. 'Tis pitiful
To court a grin, when you should woo a soul;
To break a jest, when pity would inspire
Pathetic exhortation; and to address
The skittish fancy with facetious tales,
When sent with God's commission to the heart.
So did not Paul. Direct me to a quip
Or merry turn in all he ever wrote,
And I consent you take it for your text,
Your only one, till sides and benches fail.
No: he was serious in a serious cause,
And understood too well the weighty terms
That he had ta'en in charge. He would not stoop
To conquer those by jocular exploits,
Whom truth and soberness assailed in vain.

Oh, popular applause! what heart of man
Is proof against thy sweet seducing charms?
The wisest and the best feel urgent need
Of all their caution in thy gentlest gales;
But swelled into a gust—who then, alas!
With all his canvas set, and inexpert,
And therefore heedless, can withstand thy power?
Praise from the riveled lips of toothless, bald
Decrepitude, and in the looks of lean
And craving poverty, and in the bow
Respectful of the smutched artificer,
Is oft too welcome, and may much disturb
The bias of the purpose. How much more,
Poured forth by beauty splendid and polite,
In language soft as adoration breathes?
Ah, spare your idol! think him human still;
Charms he may have, but he has frailties too;
Dote not too much, nor spoil what ye admire.

All truth is from the sempiternal source
Of light divine. But Egypt, Greece, and Rome
Drew from the stream below. More favoured, we
Drink, when we choose it, at the fountain head.
To them it flowed much mingled and defiled
With hurtful error, prejudice, and dreams
Illusive of philosophy, so called,
But falsely. Sages after sages strove,
In vain, to filter off a crystal draught
Pure from the lees, which often more enhanced
The thirst than slaked it, and not seldom bred
Intoxication and delirium wild.
In vain they pushed inquiry to the birth
And spring-time of the world; asked, Whence is man?
Why formed at all? and wherefore as he is?
Where must he find his Maker? With what rites
Adore Him? Will He hear, accept, and bless?
Or does He sit regardless of His works?
Has man within him an immortal seed?
Or does the tomb take all? If he survive
His ashes, where? and in what weal or woe?
Knots worthy of solution, which alone
A Deity could solve. Their answers vague,
And all at random, fabulous and dark,
Left them as dark themselves. Their rules of life,
Defective and unsanctioned, proved too weak
To bind the roving appetite, and lead
Blind nature to a God not yet revealed.
'Tis Revelation satisfies all doubts,
Explains all mysteries, except her own,
And so illuminates the path of life,
That fools discover it, and stray no more.
Now tell me, dignified and sapient sir,
My man of morals, nurtured in the shades
Of Academus, is this false or true?
Is Christ the abler teacher, or the schools?
If Christ, then why resort at every turn
To Athens or to Rome for wisdom short
Of man's occasions, when in Him reside
Grace, knowledge, comfort, an unfathomed store?
How oft when Paul has served us with a text,
Has Epictetus, Plato, Tully, preached!
Men that, if now alive, would sit content

And humble learners of a Saviour's worth,
Preach it who might. Such was their love of truth,
Their thirst of knowledge, and their candour too.

And thus it is. The pastor, either vain
By nature, or by flattery made so, taught
To gaze at his own splendour, and to exalt
Absurdly, not his office, but himself;
Or unenlightened, and too proud to learn,
Or vicious, and not therefore apt to teach,
Perverting often, by the stress of lewd
And loose example, whom he should instruct,
Exposes and holds up to broad disgrace
The noblest function, and discredits much
The brightest truths that man has ever seen.
For ghostly counsel, if it either fall
Below the exigence, or be not backed
With show of love, at least with hopeful proof
Of some sincerity on the giver's part;
Or be dishonoured in the exterior form
And mode of its conveyance, by such tricks
As move derision, or by foppish airs
And histrionic mummery, that let down
The pulpit to the level of the stage;
Drops from the lips a disregarded thing.
The weak perhaps are moved, but are not taught,
While prejudice in men of stronger minds
Takes deeper root, confirmed by what they see.
A relaxation of religion's hold
Upon the roving and untutored heart
Soon follows, and the curb of conscience snapt,
The laity run wild.—But do they now?
Note their extravagance, and be convinced.

As nations, ignorant of God, contrive
A wooden one, so we, no longer taught
By monitors that Mother Church supplies,
Now make our own. Posterity will ask
(If e'er posterity sees verse of mine),
Some fifty or a hundred lustrums hence,
What was a monitor in George's days?
My very gentle reader, yet unborn,
Of whom I needs must augur better things,

Since Heaven would sure grow weary of a world
Productive only of a race like us,
A monitor is wood—plank shaven thin.
We wear it at our backs. There, closely braced
And neatly fitted, it compresses hard
The prominent and most unsightly bones,
And binds the shoulders flat. We prove its use
Sovereign and most effectual to secure
A form, not now gymnastic as of yore,
From rickets and distortion, else, our lot.
But thus admonished we can walk erect,
One proof at least of manhood; while the friend
Sticks close, a Mentor worthy of his charge.
Our habits costlier than Lucullus wore,
And, by caprice as multiplied as his,
Just please us while the fashion is at full,
But change with every moon. The sycophant,
That waits to dress us, arbitrates their date,
Surveys his fair reversion with keen eye;
Finds one ill made, another obsolete,
This fits not nicely, that is ill conceived;
And, making prize of all that he condemns,
With our expenditure defrays his own.
Variety's the very spice of life,
That gives it all its flavour. We have run
Through every change that fancy, at the loom
Exhausted, has had genius to supply,
And, studious of mutation still, discard
A real elegance, a little used,
For monstrous novelty and strange disguise.
We sacrifice to dress, till household joys
And comforts cease. Dress drains our cellar dry,
And keeps our larder lean; puts out our fires,
And introduces hunger, frost, and woe,
Where peace and hospitality might reign.
What man that lives, and that knows how to live,
Would fail to exhibit at the public shows
A form as splendid as the proudest there,
Though appetite raise outcries at the cost?
A man o' the town dines late, but soon enough,
With reasonable forecast and despatch,
To ensure a side-box station at half-price.
You think, perhaps, so delicate his dress,

His daily fare as delicate. Alas!
He picks clean teeth, and, busy as he seems
With an old tavern quill, is hungry yet.
The rout is folly's circle which she draws
With magic wand. So potent is the spell,
That none decoyed into that fatal ring,
Unless by Heaven's peculiar grace, escape.
There we grow early gray, but never wise;
There form connections, and acquire no friend;
Solicit pleasure hopeless of success;
Waste youth in occupations only fit
For second childhood, and devote old age
To sports which only childhood could excuse.
There they are happiest who dissemble best
Their weariness; and they the most polite,
Who squander time and treasure with a smile,
Though at their own destruction. She that asks
Her dear five hundred friends, contemns them all,
And hates their coming. They (what can they less?)
Make just reprisals, and, with cringe and shrug
And bow obsequious, hide their hate of her.
All catch the frenzy, downward from her Grace,
Whose flambeaux flash against the morning skies,
And gild our chamber ceilings as they pass,
To her who, frugal only that her thrift
May feed excesses she can ill afford,
Is hackneyed home unlackeyed; who, in haste
Alighting, turns the key in her own door,
And, at the watchman's lantern borrowing light,
Finds a cold bed her only comfort left.
Wives beggar husbands, husbands starve their wives,
On Fortune's velvet altar offering up
Their last poor pittance—Fortune, most severe
Of goddesses yet known, and costlier far
Than all that held their routs in Juno's heaven.—
So fare we in this prison-house the world.
And 'tis a fearful spectacle to see
So many maniacs dancing in their chains.
They gaze upon the links that hold them fast
With eyes of anguish, execrate their lot,
Then shake them in despair, and dance again.

Now basket up the family of plagues
That waste our vitals. Peculation, sale
Of honour, perjury, corruption, frauds
By forgery, by subterfuge of law,
By tricks and lies, as numerous and as keen
As the necessities their authors feel;
Then cast them, closely bundled, every brat
At the right door. Profusion is its sire.
Profusion unrestrained, with all that's base
In character, has littered all the land,
And bred within the memory of no few
A priesthood such as Baal's was of old,
A people such as never was till now.
It is a hungry vice:—it eats up all
That gives society its beauty, strength,
Convenience, and security, and use;
Makes men mere vermin, worthy to be trapped
And gibbeted, as fast as catchpole claws
Can seize the slippery prey; unties the knot
Of union, and converts the sacred band
That holds mankind together to a scourge.
Profusion, deluging a state with lusts
Of grossest nature and of worst effects,
Prepares it for its ruin; hardens, blinds,
And warps the consciences of public men
Till they can laugh at virtue; mock the fools
That trust them; and, in the end, disclose a face
That would have shocked credulity herself,
Unmasked, vouchsafing this their sole excuse;—
Since all alike are selfish, why not they?
This does Profusion, and the accursed cause
Of such deep mischief has itself a cause.

In colleges and halls, in ancient days,
When learning, virtue, piety, and truth
Were precious, and inculcated with care,
There dwelt a sage called Discipline. His head,
Not yet by time completely silvered o'er,
Bespoke him past the bounds of freakish youth,
But strong for service still, and unimpaired.
His eye was meek and gentle, and a smile
Played on his lips, and in his speech was heard
Paternal sweetness, dignity, and love.

The occupation dearest to his heart
Was to encourage goodness. He would stroke
The head of modest and ingenuous worth,
That blushed at its own praise, and press the youth
Close to his side that pleased him. Learning grew
Beneath his care, a thriving, vigorous plant;
The mind was well informed, the passions held
Subordinate, and diligence was choice.
If e'er it chanced, as sometimes chance it must,
That one among so many overleaped
The limits of control, his gentle eye
Grew stern, and darted a severe rebuke;
His frown was full of terror, and his voice
Shook the delinquent with such fits of awe
As left him not, till penitence had won
Lost favour back again, and closed the breach.
But Discipline, a faithful servant long,
Declined at length into the vale of years;
A palsy struck his arm, his sparkling eye
Was quenched in rheums of age, his voice unstrung
Grew tremulous, and moved derision more
Than reverence in perverse, rebellious youth.
So colleges and halls neglected much
Their good old friend, and Discipline at length,
O'erlooked and unemployed, fell sick and died.
Then study languished, emulation slept,
And virtue fled. The schools became a scene
Of solemn farce, where ignorance in stilts,
His cap well lined with logic not his own,
With parrot tongue performed the scholar's part,
Proceeding soon a graduated dunce.
Then compromise had place, and scrutiny
Became stone-blind, precedence went in truck,
And he was competent whose purse was so.
A dissolution of all bonds ensued,
The curbs invented for the mulish mouth
Of headstrong youth were broken; bars and bolts
Grew rusty by disuse, and massy gates
Forgot their office, opening with a touch;
Till gowns at length are found mere masquerade;
The tasselled cap and the spruce band a jest,
A mockery of the world. What need of these
For gamesters, jockeys, brothellers impure,

Spendthrifts and booted sportsmen, oftener seen
With belted waist, and pointers at their heels,
Than in the bounds of duty? What was learned,
If aught was learned in childhood, is forgot,
And such expense as pinches parents blue
And mortifies the liberal hand of love,
Is squandered in pursuit of idle sports
And vicious pleasures; buys the boy a name,
That sits a stigma on his father's house,
And cleaves through life inseparably close
To him that wears it. What can after-games
Of riper joys, and commerce with the world,
The lewd vain world that must receive him soon,
Add to such erudition thus acquired,
Where science and where virtue are professed?
They may confirm his habits, rivet fast
His folly, but to spoil him is a task
That bids defiance to the united powers
Of fashion, dissipation, taverns, stews.
Now, blame we most the nurselings, or the nurse?
The children crooked and twisted and deformed
Through want of care, or her whose winking eye
And slumbering oscitancy mars the brood?
The nurse no doubt. Regardless of her charge,
She needs herself correction; needs to learn
That it is dangerous sporting with the world,
With things so sacred as a nation's trust;
The nurture of her youth, her dearest pledge.

All are not such. I had a brother once—
Peace to the memory of a man of worth,
A man of letters and of manners too—
Of manners sweet as virtue always wears,
When gay good-nature dresses her in smiles.
He graced a college in which order yet
Was sacred, and was honoured, loved, and wept,
By more than one, themselves conspicuous there.
Some minds are tempered happily, and mixt
With such ingredients of good sense and taste
Of what is excellent in man, they thirst
With such a zeal to be what they approve,
That no restraints can circumscribe them more
Than they themselves by choice, for wisdom's sake.

Nor can example hurt them. What they see
Of vice in others but enhancing more
The charms of virtue in their just esteem.
If such escape contagion, and emerge
Pure, from so foul a pool, to shine abroad,
And give the world their talents and themselves,
Small thanks to those whose negligence or sloth
Exposed their inexperience to the snare,
And left them to an undirected choice.

See, then, the quiver broken and decayed,
In which are kept our arrows. Rusting there
In wild disorder and unfit for use,
What wonder if discharged into the world
They shame their shooters with a random flight,
Their points obtuse and feathers drunk with wine.
Well may the Church wage unsuccessful war
With such artillery armed. Vice parries wide
The undreaded volley with a sword of straw,
And stands an impudent and fearless mark.

Have we not tracked the felon home, and found
His birthplace and his dam? The country mourns—
Mourns, because every plague that can infest
Society, that saps and worms the base
Of the edifice that Policy has raised,
Swarms in all quarters; meets the eye, the ear,
And suffocates the breath at every turn.
Profusion breeds them. And the cause itself
Of that calamitous mischief has been found,
Found, too, where most offensive, in the skirts
Of the robed pedagogue. Else, let the arraigned
Stand up unconscious and refute the charge.
So, when the Jewish leader stretched his arm
And waved his rod divine, a race obscene,
Spawned in the muddy beds of Nile, came forth
Polluting Egypt. Gardens, fields, and plains
Were covered with the pest. The streets were filled;
The croaking nuisance lurked in every nook,
Nor palaces nor even chambers 'scaped,
And the land stank, so numerous was the fry.

BOOK III.

THE GARDEN.

As one who, long in thickets and in brakes
Entangled, winds now this way and now that
His devious course uncertain, seeking home;
Or, having long in miry ways been foiled
And sore discomfited, from slough to slough
Plunging, and half despairing of escape,
If chance at length he find a greensward smooth
And faithful to the foot, his spirits rise,
He chirrups brisk his ear-erecting steed,
And winds his way with pleasure and with ease;
So I, designing other themes, and called
To adorn the Sofa with eulogium due,
To tell its slumbers and to paint its dreams,
Have rambled wide. In country, city, seat
Of academic fame, howe'er deserved,
Long held, and scarcely disengaged at last.
But now with pleasant pace, a cleanlier road
I mean to tread. I feel myself at large,
Courageous, and refreshed for future toil,
If toil await me, or if dangers new.

Since pulpits fail, and sounding-boards reflect
Most part an empty ineffectual sound,
What chance that I, to fame so little known,
Nor conversant with men or manners much,
Should speak to purpose, or with better hope
Crack the satiric thong? 'Twere wiser far
For me, enamoured of sequestered scenes,
And charmed with rural beauty, to repose,
Where chance may throw me, beneath elm or vine
My languid limbs, when summer sears the plains;
Or when rough winter rages, on the soft
And sheltered Sofa, while the nitrous air
Feeds a blue flame and makes a cheerful hearth;
There, undisturbed by folly, and apprised
How great the danger of disturbing her,
To muse in silence, or at least confine
Remarks that gall so many to the few,

My partners in retreat. Disgust concealed
Is ofttimes proof of wisdom, when the fault
Is obstinate, and cure beyond our reach.

Domestic happiness, thou only bliss
Of Paradise that has survived the fall!
Though few now taste thee unimpaired and pure,
Or, tasting, long enjoy thee, too infirm
Or too incautious to preserve thy sweets
Unmixed with drops of bitter, which neglect
Or temper sheds into thy crystal cup.
Thou art the nurse of virtue. In thine arms
She smiles, appearing, as in truth she is,
Heaven-born, and destined to the skies again.
Thou art not known where Pleasure is adored,
That reeling goddess with the zoneless waist
And wandering eyes, still leaning on the arm
Of Novelty, her fickle frail support;
For thou art meek and constant, hating change,
And finding in the calm of truth-tried love
Joys that her stormy raptures never yield.
Forsaking thee, what shipwreck have we made
Of honour, dignity, and fair renown,
Till prostitution elbows us aside
In all our crowded streets, and senates seem
Convened for purposes of empire less,
Than to release the adult'ress from her bond.
The adult'ress! what a theme for angry verse,
What provocation to the indignant heart
That feels for injured love! but I disdain
The nauseous task to paint her as she is,
Cruel, abandoned, glorying in her shame.
No; let her pass, and charioted along
In guilty splendour shake the public ways;
The frequency of crimes has washed them white,
And verse of mine shall never brand the wretch
Whom matrons now of character unsmirched
And chaste themselves, are not ashamed to own.
Virtue and vice had boundaries in old time
Not to be passed; and she that had renounced
Her sex's honour, was renounced herself
By all that prized it; not for prudery's sake,
But dignity's, resentful of the wrong.

'Twas hard, perhaps, on here and there a waif
Desirous to return, and not received;
But was a wholesome rigour in the main,
And taught the unblemished to preserve with care
That purity, whose loss was loss of all.
Men, too, were nice in honour in those days,
And judged offenders well. Then he that sharped,
And pocketed a prize by fraud obtained,
Was marked and shunned as odious. He that sold
His country, or was slack when she required
His every nerve in action and at stretch,
Paid with the blood that he had basely spared
The price of his default. But now,—yes, now,
We are become so candid and so fair,
So liberal in construction, and so rich
In Christian charity (good-natured age!)
That they are safe, sinners of either sex,
Transgress what laws they may. Well dressed, well bred,
Well equipaged, is ticket good enough
To pass us readily through every door.
Hypocrisy, detest her as we may
(And no man's hatred ever wronged her yet),
May claim this merit still—that she admits
The worth of what she mimics with such care,
And thus gives virtue indirect applause;
But she has burnt her mask, not needed here,
Where vice has such allowance, that her shifts
And specious semblances have lost their use.

I was a stricken deer that left the herd
Long since; with many an arrow deep infixt
My panting side was charged, when I withdrew
To seek a tranquil death in distant shades.
There was I found by one who had himself
Been hurt by the archers. In his side he bore,
And in his hands and feet, the cruel scars.
With gentle force soliciting the darts
He drew them forth, and healed and bade me live.
Since then, with few associates, in remote
And silent woods I wander, far from those
My former partners of the peopled scene,
With few associates, and not wishing more.
Here much I ruminate, as much I may,

With other views of men and manners now
Than once, and others of a life to come.
I see that all are wanderers, gone astray
Each in his own delusions; they are lost
In chase of fancied happiness, still woo'd
And never won. Dream after dream ensues,
And still they dream that they shall still succeed,
And still are disappointed: rings the world
With the vain stir. I sum up half mankind,
And add two-thirds of the remaining half,
And find the total of their hopes and fears
Dreams, empty dreams. The million flit as gay
As if created only, like the fly
That spreads his motley wings in the eye of noon,
To sport their season and be seen no more.
The rest are sober dreamers, grave and wise,
And pregnant with discoveries new and rare.
Some write a narrative of wars, and feats
Of heroes little known, and call the rant
A history; describe the man, of whom
His own coevals took but little note,
And paint his person, character, and views,
As they had known him from his mother's womb;
They disentangle from the puzzled skein,
In which obscurity has wrapped them up,
The threads of politic and shrewd design
That ran through all his purposes, and charge
His mind with meanings that he never had,
Or, having, kept concealed. Some drill and bore
The solid earth, and from the strata there
Extract a register, by which we learn
That He who made it and revealed its date
To Moses, was mistaken in its age.
Some, more acute and more industrious still,
Contrive creation; travel nature up
To the sharp peak of her sublimest height,
And tell us whence the stars; why some are fixt,
And planetary some; what gave them first
Rotation, from what fountain flowed their light.
Great contest follows, and much learned dust
Involves the combatants, each claiming truth,
And truth disclaiming both. And thus they spend
The little wick of life's poor shallow lamp

In playing tricks with nature, giving laws
To distant worlds, and trifling in their own.
Is't not a pity now, that tickling rheums
Should ever tease the lungs and blear the sight
Of oracles like these? Great pity, too,
That having wielded the elements, and built
A thousand systems, each in his own way,
They should go out in fume and be forgot?
Ah, what is life thus spent? and what are they
But frantic who thus spend it? all for smoke—
Eternity for bubbles proves at last
A senseless bargain. When I see such games
Played by the creatures of a Power who swears
That He will judge the earth, and call the fool
To a sharp reckoning that has lived in vain,
And when I weigh this seeming wisdom well,
And prove it in the infallible result
So hollow and so false—I feel my heart
Dissolve in pity, and account the learned,
If this be learning, most of all deceived.
Great crimes alarm the conscience, but it sleeps
While thoughtful man is plausibly amused.
Defend me, therefore, common sense, say I,
From reveries so airy, from the toil
Of dropping buckets into empty wells,
And growing old in drawing nothing up!

'Twere well, says one sage erudite, profound,
Terribly arched and aquiline his nose,
And overbuilt with most impending brows,
'Twere well could you permit the world to live
As the world pleases. What's the world to you?—
Much. I was born of woman, and drew milk
As sweet as charity from human breasts.
I think, articulate, I laugh and weep,
And exercise all functions of a man.
How then should I and any man that lives
Be strangers to each other? Pierce my vein,
Take of the crimson stream meandering there,
And catechise it well. Apply your glass,
Search it, and prove now if it be not blood
Congenial with thine own; and if it be,
What edge of subtlety canst thou suppose

Keen enough, wise and skilful as thou art,
To cut the link of brotherhood, by which
One common Maker bound me to the kind?
True; I am no proficient, I confess,
In arts like yours. I cannot call the swift
And perilous lightnings from the angry clouds,
And bid them hide themselves in the earth beneath;
I cannot analyse the air, nor catch
The parallax of yonder luminous point
That seems half quenched in the immense abyss:
Such powers I boast not—neither can I rest
A silent witness of the headlong rage,
Or heedless folly, by which thousands die,
Bone of my bone, and kindred souls to mine.

God never meant that man should scale the heavens
By strides of human wisdom. In His works,
Though wondrous, He commands us in His Word
To seek Him rather where His mercy shines.
The mind indeed, enlightened from above,
Views Him in all; ascribes to the grand cause
The grand effect; acknowledges with joy
His manner, and with rapture tastes His style.
But never yet did philosophic tube,
That brings the planets home into the eye
Of observation, and discovers, else
Not visible, His family of worlds,
Discover Him that rules them; such a veil
Hangs over mortal eyes, blind from the birth,
And dark in things divine. Full often too
Our wayward intellect, the more we learn
Of nature, overlooks her Author more;
From instrumental causes proud to draw
Conclusions retrograde, and mad mistake:
But if His Word once teach us, shoot a ray
Through all the heart's dark chambers, and reveal
Truths undiscerned but by that holy light,
Then all is plain. Philosophy, baptised
In the pure fountain of eternal love,
Has eyes indeed; and, viewing all she sees
As meant to indicate a God to man,
Gives HIM His praise, and forfeits not her own.
Learning has borne such fruit in other days

On all her branches. Piety has found
Friends in the friends of science, and true prayer
Has flowed from lips wet with Castalian dews.
Such was thy wisdom, Newton, childlike sage!
Sagacious reader of the works of God,
And in His Word sagacious. Such too thine,
Milton, whose genius had angelic wings,
And fed on manna. And such thine, in whom
Our British Themis gloried with just cause,
Immortal Hale! for deep discernment praised,
And sound integrity not more, than famed
For sanctity of manners undefiled.

All flesh is grass, and all its glory fades
Like the fair flower dishevelled in the wind;
Riches have wings, and grandeur is a dream;
The man we celebrate must find a tomb,
And we that worship him, ignoble graves.
Nothing is proof against the general curse
Of vanity, that seizes all below.
The only amaranthine flower on earth
Is virtue; the only lasting treasure, truth.
But what is truth? 'twas Pilate's question put
To truth itself, that deigned him no reply.
And wherefore? will not God impart His light
To them that ask it?—Freely—'tis His joy,
His glory, and His nature to impart.
But to the proud, uncandid, insincere,
Or negligent inquirer, not a spark.
What's that which brings contempt upon a book
And him that writes it, though the style be neat,
The method clear, and argument exact?
That makes a minister in holy things
The joy of many, and the dread of more,
His name a theme for praise and for reproach?—
That, while it gives us worth in God's account,
Depreciates and undoes us in our own?
What pearl is it that rich men cannot buy,
That learning is too proud to gather up,
But which the poor and the despised of all
Seek and obtain, and often find unsought?
Tell me, and I will tell thee what is truth.

Oh, friendly to the best pursuits of man,
Friendly to thought, to virtue, and to peace,
Domestic life in rural leisure passed!
Few know thy value, and few taste thy sweets,
Though many boast thy favours, and affect
To understand and choose thee for their own.
But foolish man foregoes his proper bliss,
Even as his first progenitor, and quits,
Though placed in paradise, for earth has still
Some traces of her youthful beauty left,
Substantial happiness for transient joy.
Scenes formed for contemplation, and to nurse
The growing seeds of wisdom; that suggest,
By every pleasing image they present,
Reflections such as meliorate the heart,
Compose the passions, and exalt the mind;
Scenes such as these, 'tis his supreme delight
To fill with riot and defile with blood.
Should some contagion, kind to the poor brutes
We persecute, annihilate the tribes
That draw the sportsman over hill and dale
Fearless, and rapt away from all his cares;
Should never game-fowl hatch her eggs again,
Nor baited hook deceive the fish's eye;
Could pageantry, and dance, and feast, and song
Be quelled in all our summer months' retreats;
How many self-deluded nymphs and swains,
Who dream they have a taste for fields and groves,
Would find them hideous nurseries of the spleen,
And crowd the roads, impatient for the town!
They love the country, and none else, who seek
For their own sake its silence and its shade;
Delights which who would leave, that has a heart
Susceptible of pity, or a mind
Cultured and capable of sober thought,
For all the savage din of the swift pack,
And clamours of the field? Detested sport,
That owes its pleasures to another's pain,
That feeds upon the sobs and dying shrieks
Of harmless nature, dumb, but yet endued
With eloquence, that agonies inspire,
Of silent tears and heart-distending sighs!
Vain tears, alas! and sighs that never find

A corresponding tone in jovial souls.
Well—one at least is safe. One sheltered hare
Has never heard the sanguinary yell
Of cruel man, exulting in her woes.
Innocent partner of my peaceful home,
Whom ten long years' experience of my care
Has made at last familiar, she has lost
Much of her vigilant instinctive dread,
Not needful here, beneath a roof like mine.
Yes—thou mayst eat thy bread, and lick the hand
That feeds thee; thou mayst frolic on the floor
At evening, and at night retire secure
To thy straw-couch, and slumber unalarmed;
For I have gained thy confidence, have pledged
All that is human in me to protect
Thine unsuspecting gratitude and love.
If I survive thee I will dig thy grave,
And when I place thee in it, sighing say,
I knew at least one hare that had a friend.

How various his employments, whom the world
Calls idle, and who justly in return
Esteems that busy world an idler, too!
Friends, books, a garden, and perhaps his pen,
Delightful industry enjoyed at home,
And nature in her cultivated trim
Dressed to his taste, inviting him abroad—
Can he want occupation who has these?
Will he be idle who has much to enjoy?
Me, therefore, studious of laborious ease,
Not slothful; happy to deceive the time,
Not waste it; and aware that human life
Is but a loan to be repaid with use,
When He shall call His debtors to account,
From whom are all our blessings; business finds
Even here: while sedulous I seek to improve,
At least neglect not, or leave unemployed,
The mind He gave me; driving it, though slack
Too oft, and much impeded in its work
By causes not to be divulged in vain,
To its just point—the service of mankind.
He that attends to his interior self,
That has a heart and keeps it; has a mind

That hungers and supplies it; and who seeks
A social, not a dissipated life,
Has business; feels himself engaged to achieve
No unimportant, though a silent task.
A life all turbulence and noise may seem,
To him that leads it, wise and to be praised;
But wisdom is a pearl with most success
Sought in still water, and beneath clear skies.
He that is ever occupied in storms,
Or dives not for it or brings up instead,
Vainly industrious, a disgraceful prize.

The morning finds the self-sequestered man
Fresh for his task, intend what task he may.
Whether inclement seasons recommend
His warm but simple home, where he enjoys,
With her who shares his pleasures and his heart,
Sweet converse, sipping calm the fragrant lymph
Which neatly she prepares; then to his book
Well chosen, and not sullenly perused
In selfish silence, but imparted oft
As aught occurs that she may smile to hear,
Or turn to nourishment digested well.
Or if the garden with its many cares,
All well repaid, demand him, he attends
The welcome call, conscious how much the hand
Of lubbard labour needs his watchful eye,
Oft loitering lazily if not o'erseen,
Or misapplying his unskilful strength.
Nor does he govern only or direct,
But much performs himself; no works indeed
That ask robust tough sinews, bred to toil,
Servile employ—but such as may amuse,
Not tire, demanding rather skill than force.
Proud of his well-spread walls, he views his trees
That meet, no barren interval between,
With pleasure more than even their fruits afford,
Which, save himself who trains them, none can feel.
These, therefore, are his own peculiar charge,
No meaner hand may discipline the shoots,
None but his steel approach them. What is weak,
Distempered, or has lost prolific powers,
Impaired by age, his unrelenting hand

Dooms to the knife. Nor does he spare the soft
And succulent that feeds its giant growth,
But barren, at the expense of neighbouring twigs
Less ostentatious, and yet studded thick
With hopeful gems. The rest, no portion left
That may disgrace his art, or disappoint
Large expectation, he disposes neat
At measured distances, that air and sun
Admitted freely may afford their aid,
And ventilate and warm the swelling buds.
Hence Summer has her riches, Autumn hence,
And hence even Winter fills his withered hand
With blushing fruits, and plenty not his own,
Fair recompense of labour well bestowed
And wise precaution, which a clime so rude
Makes needful still, whose Spring is but the child
Of churlish Winter, in her froward moods
Discovering much the temper of her sire.
For oft, as if in her the stream of mild
Maternal nature had reversed its course,
She brings her infants forth with many smiles,
But, once delivered, kills them with a frown.
He therefore, timely warned, himself supplies
Her want of care, screening and keeping warm
The plenteous bloom, that no rough blast may sweep
His garlands from the boughs. Again, as oft
As the sun peeps and vernal airs breathe mild,
The fence withdrawn, he gives them ev'ry beam,
And spreads his hopes before the blaze of day.

To raise the prickly and green-coated gourd,
So grateful to the palate, and when rare
So coveted, else base and disesteemed —
Food for the vulgar merely — is an art
That toiling ages have but just matured,
And at this moment unessayed in song.
Yet gnats have had, and frogs and mice long since,
Their eulogy; those sang the Mantuan bard,
And these the Grecian in ennobling strains;
And in thy numbers, Philips, shines for aye
The solitary Shilling. Pardon then,
Ye sage dispensers of poetic fame!
The ambition of one meaner far, whose powers

Presuming an attempt not less sublime,
Pant for the praise of dressing to the taste
Of critic appetite, no sordid fare,
A cucumber, while costly yet and scarce.

The stable yields a stercoraceous heap
Impregnated with quick fermenting salts,
And potent to resist the freezing blast.
For ere the beech and elm have cast their leaf
Deciduous, and when now November dark
Checks vegetation in the torpid plant
Exposed to his cold breath, the task begins.
Warily therefore, and with prudent heed
He seeks a favoured spot, that where he builds
The agglomerated pile, his frame may front
The sun's meridian disk, and at the back
Enjoy close shelter, wall, or reeds, or hedge
Impervious to the wind. First he bids spread
Dry fern or littered hay, that may imbibe
The ascending damps; then leisurely impose,
And lightly, shaking it with agile hand
From the full fork, the saturated straw.
What longest binds the closest, forms secure
The shapely side, that as it rises takes
By just degrees an overhanging breadth,
Sheltering the base with its projected eaves.
The uplifted frame compact at every joint,
And overlaid with clear translucent glass,
He settles next upon the sloping mount,
Whose sharp declivity shoots off secure
From the dashed pane the deluge as it falls.
He shuts it close, and the first labour ends.
Thrice must the voluble and restless earth
Spin round upon her axle, ere the warmth
Slow gathering in the midst, through the square mass
Diffused, attain the surface. When, behold!
A pestilent and most corrosive steam,
Like a gross fog Boeotian, rising fast,
And fast condensed upon the dewy sash,
Asks egress; which obtained, the overcharged
And drenched conservatory breathes abroad,
In volumes wheeling slow, the vapour dank,
And purified, rejoices to have lost

Its foul inhabitant. But to assuage
The impatient fervour which it first conceives
Within its reeking bosom, threatening death
To his young hopes, requires discreet delay.
Experience, slow preceptress, teaching oft
The way to glory by miscarriage foul,
Must prompt him, and admonish how to catch
The auspicious moment, when the tempered heat,
Friendly to vital motion, may afford
Soft fermentation, and invite the seed.
The seed selected wisely, plump and smooth
And glossy, he commits to pots of size
Diminutive, well filled with well-prepared
And fruitful soil, that has been treasured long,
And drunk no moisture from the dripping clouds:
These on the warm and genial earth that hides
The smoking manure, and o'erspreads it all,
He places lightly, and, as time subdues
The rage of fermentation, plunges deep
In the soft medium, till they stand immersed.
Then rise the tender germs upstarting quick
And spreading wide their spongy lobes; at first
Pale, wan, and livid; but assuming soon,
If fanned by balmy and nutritious air
Strained through the friendly mats, a vivid green.
Two leaves produced, two rough indented leaves,
Cautious he pinches from the second stalk
A pimple, that portends a future sprout,
And interdicts its growth. Thence straight succeed
The branches, sturdy to his utmost wish,
Prolific all, and harbingers of more.
The crowded roots demand enlargement now
And transplantation in an ampler space.
Indulged in what they wish, they soon supply
Large foliage, overshadowing golden flowers,
Blown on the summit of the apparent fruit.
These have their sexes, and when summer shines
The bee transports the fertilising meal
From flower to flower, and even the breathing air
Wafts the rich prize to its appointed use.
Not so when winter scowls. Assistant art
Then acts in nature's office, brings to pass
The glad espousals and insures the crop.

Grudge not, ye rich (since luxury must have
His dainties, and the world's more numerous half
Lives by contriving delicates for you),
Grudge not the cost. Ye little know the cares,
The vigilance, the labour, and the skill
That day and night are exercised, and hang
Upon the ticklish balance of suspense,
That ye may garnish your profuse regales
With summer fruits, brought forth by wintry suns.
Ten thousand dangers lie in wait to thwart
The process. Heat and cold, and wind and steam,
Moisture and drought, mice, worms, and swarming flies
Minute as dust and numberless, oft work
Dire disappointment that admits no cure,
And which no care can obviate. It were long,
Too long to tell the expedients and the shifts
Which he, that fights a season so severe,
Devises, while he guards his tender trust,
And oft, at last, in vain. The learned and wise
Sarcastic would exclaim, and judge the song
Cold as its theme, and, like its theme, the fruit
Of too much labour, worthless when produced.

Who loves a garden, loves a greenhouse too.
Unconscious of a less propitious clime
There blooms exotic beauty, warm and snug,
While the winds whistle and the snows descend.
The spiry myrtle with unwithering leaf
Shines there and flourishes. The golden boast
Of Portugal and Western India there,
The ruddier orange and the paler lime,
Peep through their polished foliage at the storm,
And seem to smile at what they need not fear.
The amomum there with intermingling flowers
And cherries hangs her twigs. Geranium boasts
Her crimson honours, and the spangled beau,
Ficoides, glitters bright the winter long,
All plants, of every leaf, that can endure
The winter's frown if screened from his shrewd bite,
Live there and prosper. Those Ausonia claims,
Levantine regions these; the Azores send
Their jessamine; her jessamine remote
Caffraria: foreigners from many lands,

They form one social shade, as if convened
By magic summons of the Orphean lyre.
Yet such arrangement, rarely brought to pass
But by a master's hand, disposing well
The gay diversities of leaf and flower,
Must lend its aid to illustrate all their charms,
And dress the regular yet various scene.
Plant behind plant aspiring, in the van
The dwarfish, in the rear retired, but still
Sublime above the rest, the statelier stand.
So once were ranged the sons of ancient Rome,
A noble show, while Roscius trod the stage;
And so, while Garrick, as renowned as he,
The sons of Albion, fearing each to lose
Some note of Nature's music from his lips,
And covetous of Shakespeare's beauty, seen
In every flash of his far-beaming eye.
Nor taste alone and well-contrived display
Suffice to give the marshalled ranks the grace
Of their complete effect. Much yet remains
Unsung, and many cares are yet behind
And more laborious; cares on which depends
Their vigour, injured soon, not soon restored.
The soil must be renewed, which often washed
Loses its treasure of salubrious salts,
And disappoints the roots; the slender roots,
Close interwoven where they meet the vase,
Must smooth be shorn away; the sapless branch
Must fly before the knife; the withered leaf
Must be detached, and where it strews the floor
Swept with a woman's neatness, breeding else
Contagion, and disseminating death.
Discharge but these kind offices (and who
Would spare, that loves them, offices like these?)
Well they reward the toil. The sight is pleased,
The scent regaled, each odoriferous leaf,
Each opening blossom, freely breathes abroad
Its gratitude, and thanks him with its sweets.

So manifold, all pleasing in their kind,
All healthful, are the employs of rural life,
Reiterated as the wheel of time
Runs round, still ending, and beginning still.

Nor are these all. To deck the shapely knoll
That, softly swelled and gaily dressed, appears
A flowery island from the dark green lawn
Emerging, must be deemed a labour due
To no mean hand, and asks the touch of taste.
Here also grateful mixture of well-matched
And sorted hues (each giving each relief,
And by contrasted beauty shining more)
Is needful. Strength may wield the ponderous spade,
May turn the clod, and wheel the compost home,
But elegance, chief grace the garden shows
And most attractive, is the fair result
Of thought, the creature of a polished mind.
Without it, all is Gothic as the scene
To which the insipid citizen resorts,
Near yonder heath; where industry misspent,
But proud of his uncouth, ill-chosen task,
Has made a heaven on earth; with suns and moons
Of close-rammed stones has charged the encumbered soil,
And fairly laid the zodiac in the dust.
He, therefore, who would see his flowers disposed
Sightly and in just order, ere he gives
The beds the trusted treasure of their seeds,
Forecasts the future whole; that when the scene
Shall break into its preconceived display,
Each for itself, and all as with one voice
Conspiring, may attest his bright design.
Nor even then, dismissing as performed
His pleasant work, may he suppose it done.
Few self-supported flowers endure the wind
Uninjured, but expect the upholding aid
Of the smooth-shaven prop, and neatly tied
Are wedded thus, like beauty to old age,
For interest sake, the living to the dead.
Some clothe the soil that feeds them, far diffused
And lowly creeping, modest and yet fair;
Like virtue, thriving most where little seen.
Some, more aspiring, catch the neighbour shrub
With clasping tendrils, and invest his branch,
Else unadorned, with many a gay festoon
And fragrant chaplet, recompensing well
The strength they borrow with the grace they lend.
All hate the rank society of weeds,

Noisome, and very greedy to exhaust
The impoverished earth; an overbearing race,
That, like the multitude made faction-mad,
Disturb good order, and degrade true worth.

Oh blest seclusion from a jarring world,
Which he, thus occupied, enjoys! Retreat
Cannot, indeed, to guilty man restore
Lost innocence, or cancel follies past;
But it has peace, and much secures the mind
From all assaults of evil; proving still
A faithful barrier, not o'erleaped with ease
By vicious custom raging uncontrolled
Abroad and desolating public life.
When fierce temptation, seconded within
By traitor appetite, and armed with darts
Tempered in hell, invades the throbbing breast,
To combat may be glorious, and success
Perhaps may crown us, but to fly is safe.
Had I the choice of sublunary good,
What could I wish that I possess not here?
Health, leisure; means to improve it, friendship, peace,
No loose or wanton though a wandering muse,
And constant occupation without care.
Thus blest, I draw a picture of that bliss;
Hopeless, indeed, that dissipated minds
And profligate abusers of a world
Created fair so much in vain for them,
Should seek the guiltless joys that I describe,
Allured by my report; but sure no less
That self-condemned they must neglect the prize,
And what they will not taste, must yet approve.
What we admire we praise; and when we praise
Advance it into notice, that, its worth
Acknowledged, others may admire it too.
I therefore recommend, though at the risk
Of popular disgust, yet boldly still,
The cause of piety and sacred truth
And virtue, and those scenes which God ordained
Should best secure them and promote them most;
Scenes that I love, and with regret perceive
Forsaken, or through folly not enjoyed.
Pure is the nymph, though liberal of her smiles,

And chaste, though unconfined, whom I extol.
Not as the prince in Shushan, when he called,
Vain-glorious of her charms, his Vashti forth,
To grace the full pavilion. His design
Was but to boast his own peculiar good,
Which all might view with envy, none partake.
My charmer is not mine alone; my sweets,
And she that sweetens all my bitters, too,
Nature, enchanting Nature, in whose form
And lineaments divine I trace a hand
That errs not, and find raptures still renewed,
Is free to all men — universal prize.
Strange that so fair a creature should yet want
Admirers, and be destined to divide
With meaner objects even the few she finds.
Stript of her ornaments, her leaves and flowers,
She loses all her influence. Cities then
Attract us, and neglected Nature pines,
Abandoned, as unworthy of our love.
But are not wholesome airs, though unperfumed
By roses, and clear suns, though scarcely felt,
And groves, if unharmonious yet secure
From clamour and whose very silence charms,
To be preferred to smoke — to the eclipse
That Metropolitan volcanoes make,
Whose Stygian throats breathe darkness all day long,
And to the stir of commerce, driving slow,
And thundering loud with his ten thousand wheels?
They would be, were not madness in the head
And folly in the heart; were England now
What England was, plain, hospitable, kind,
And undebauched. But we have bid farewell
To all the virtues of those better days,
And all their honest pleasures. Mansions once
Knew their own masters, and laborious hands
That had survived the father, served the son.
Now the legitimate and rightful lord
Is but a transient guest, newly arrived
And soon to be supplanted. He that saw
His patrimonial timber cast its leaf,
Sells the last scantling, and transfers the price
To some shrewd sharper, ere it buds again.
Estates are landscapes, gazed upon awhile,

Then advertised, and auctioneered away.
The country starves, and they that feed the o'er-charged
And surfeited lewd town with her fair dues,
By a just judgment strip and starve themselves.
The wings that waft our riches out of sight
Grow on the gamester's elbows, and the alert
And nimble motion of those restless joints,
That never tire, soon fans them all away.
Improvement too, the idol of the age,
Is fed with many a victim. Lo! he comes—
The omnipotent magician, Brown, appears.
Down falls the venerable pile, the abode
Of our forefathers, a grave whiskered race,
But tasteless. Springs a palace in its stead,
But in a distant spot; where more exposed
It may enjoy the advantage of the North
And aguish East, till time shall have transformed
Those naked acres to a sheltering grove.
He speaks. The lake in front becomes a lawn,
Woods vanish, hills subside, and valleys rise,
And streams, as if created for his use,
Pursue the track of his directed wand
Sinuous or straight, now rapid and now slow,
Now murmuring soft, now roaring in cascades,
Even as he bids. The enraptured owner smiles.
'Tis finished. And yet, finished as it seems,
Still wants a grace, the loveliest it could show,
A mine to satisfy the enormous cost.
Drained to the last poor item of his wealth,
He sighs, departs, and leaves the accomplished plan
That he has touched and retouched, many a day
Laboured, and many a night pursued in dreams,
Just when it meets his hopes, and proves the heaven
He wanted, for a wealthier to enjoy.
And now perhaps the glorious hour is come,
When having no stake left, no pledge to endear
Her interests, or that gives her sacred cause
A moment's operation on his love,
He burns with most intense and flagrant zeal
To serve his country. Ministerial grace
Deals him out money from the public chest,
Or, if that mine be shut, some private purse
Supplies his need with an usurious loan,

To be refunded duly, when his vote,
Well-managed, shall have earned its worthy price.
Oh, innocent compared with arts like these,
Crape and cocked pistol and the whistling ball
Sent through the traveller's temples! He that finds
One drop of heaven's sweet mercy in his cup,
Can dig, beg, rot, and perish well-content,
So he may wrap himself in honest rags
At his last gasp; but could not for a world
Fish up his dirty and dependent bread
From pools and ditches of the commonwealth,
Sordid and sickening at his own success.

Ambition, avarice, penury incurred
By endless riot, vanity, the lust
Of pleasure and variety, despatch,
As duly as the swallows disappear,
The world of wandering knights and squires to town;
London engulfs them all. The shark is there,
And the shark's prey; the spendthrift, and the leech
That sucks him. There the sycophant, and he
That with bare-headed and obsequious bows
Begs a warm office, doomed to a cold jail
And groat per diem if his patron frown.
The levee swarms, as if in golden pomp
Were charactered on every statesman's door,
'BATTERED AND BANKRUPT FORTUNES MENDED HERE.'
These are the charms that sully and eclipse
The charms of nature. 'Tis the cruel gripe
That lean hard-handed poverty inflicts,
The hope of better things, the chance to win,
The wish to shine, the thirst to be amused,
That, at the sound of Winter's hoary wing,
Unpeople all our counties of such herds
Of fluttering, loitering, cringing, begging, loose
And wanton vagrants, as make London, vast
And boundless as it is, a crowded coop.

Oh thou resort and mart of all the earth,
Chequered with all complexions of mankind,
And spotted with all crimes; in whom I see
Much that I love, and more that I admire,
And all that I abhor; thou freckled fair

That pleases and yet shocks me, I can laugh
And I can weep, can hope, and can despond,
Feel wrath and pity when I think on thee!
Ten righteous would have saved a city once,
And thou hast many righteous.—Well for thee—
That salt preserves thee; more corrupted else,
And therefore more obnoxious at this hour
Than Sodom in her day had power to be,
For whom God heard his Abram plead in vain.

BOOK IV.

THE WINTER EVENING.

Hark! 'tis the twanging horn o'er yonder bridge,
That with its wearisome but needful length
Bestrides the wintry flood, in which the moon
Sees her unwrinkled face reflected bright;—
He comes, the herald of a noisy world,
With spattered boots, strapped waist, and frozen locks,
News from all nations lumbering at his back.
True to his charge the close-packed load behind,
Yet careless what he brings, his one concern
Is to conduct it to the destined inn,
And, having dropped the expected bag—pass on.
He whistles as he goes, light-hearted wretch,
Cold and yet cheerful: messenger of grief
Perhaps to thousands, and of joy to some;
To him indifferent whether grief or joy.
Houses in ashes, and the fall of stocks,
Births, deaths, and marriages, epistles wet
With tears that trickled down the writer's cheeks,
Fast as the periods from his fluent quill,
Or charged with amorous sighs of absent swains,
Or nymphs responsive, equally affect
His horse and him, unconscious of them all.
But oh, the important budget! ushered in
With such heart-shaking music, who can say
What are its tidings? have our troops awaked?
Or do they still, as if with opium drugged,
Snore to the murmurs of the Atlantic wave?
Is India free? and does she wear her plumed
And jewelled turban with a smile of peace,
Or do we grind her still? The grand debate,
The popular harangue, the tart reply,
The logic and the wisdom and the wit
And the loud laugh—I long to know them all;
I burn to set the imprisoned wranglers free,
And give them voice and utterance once again.

Now stir the fire, and close the shutters fast,
Let fall the curtains, wheel the sofa round,

And while the bubbling and loud-hissing urn
Throws up a steamy column, and the cups,
That cheer but not inebriate, wait on each,
So let us welcome peaceful evening in.
Not such his evening, who with shining face
Sweats in the crowded theatre, and squeezed
And bored with elbow-points through both his sides,
Outscolds the ranting actor on the stage;
Nor his, who patient stands till his feet throb
And his head thumps, to feed upon the breath
Of patriots bursting with heroic rage,
Or placemen all tranquillity and smiles.
This folio of four pages, happy work!
Which not even critics criticise, that holds
Inquisitive attention while I read
Fast bound in chains of silence, which the fair,
Though eloquent themselves, yet fear to break,
What is it but a map of busy life,
Its fluctuations and its vast concerns?
Here runs the mountainous and craggy ridge
That tempts ambition. On the summit, see,
The seals of office glitter in his eyes;
He climbs, he pants, he grasps them. At his heels,
Close at his heels, a demagogue ascends,
And with a dextrous jerk soon twists him down
And wins them, but to lose them in his turn.
Here rills of oily eloquence, in soft
Meanders, lubricate the course they take;
The modest speaker is ashamed and grieved
To engross a moment's notice, and yet begs,
Begs a propitious ear for his poor thoughts,
However trivial all that he conceives.
Sweet bashfulness! it claims, at least, this praise,
The dearth of information and good sense
That it foretells us, always comes to pass.
Cataracts of declamation thunder here,
There forests of no meaning spread the page
In which all comprehension wanders lost;
While fields of pleasantry amuse us there,
With merry descants on a nation's woes.
The rest appears a wilderness of strange
But gay confusion; roses for the cheeks
And lilies for the brows of faded age,

Teeth for the toothless, ringlets for the bald,
Heaven, earth, and ocean plundered of their sweets.
Nectareous essences, Olympian dews,
Sermons and city feasts and favourite airs,
Ethereal journeys, submarine exploits,
And Katterfelto with his hair on end
At his own wonders, wondering for his bread.

'Tis pleasant through the loopholes of retreat
To peep at such a world; to see the stir
Of the great Babel and not feel the crowd;
To hear the roar she sends through all her gates
At a safe distance, where the dying sound
Falls a soft murmur on the uninjured ear.
Thus sitting and surveying thus at ease
The globe and its concerns, I seem advanced
To some secure and more than mortal height,
That liberates and exempts me from them all.
It turns submitted to my view, turns round
With all its generations; I behold
The tumult and am still. The sound of war
Has lost its terrors ere it reaches me;
Grieves, but alarms me not. I mourn the pride
And avarice that makes man a wolf to man;
Hear the faint echo of those brazen throats
By which he speaks the language of his heart,
And sigh, but never tremble at the sound.
He travels and expatiates, as the bee
From flower to flower so he from land to land;
The manners, customs, policy of all
Pay contribution to the store he gleans,
He sucks intelligence in every clime,
And spreads the honey of his deep research
At his return—a rich repast for me.
He travels and I too. I tread his deck,
Ascend his topmast, through his peering eyes
Discover countries, with a kindred heart
Suffer his woes and share in his escapes;
While fancy, like the finger of a clock,
Runs the great circuit, and is still at home.

Oh Winter, ruler of the inverted year,
Thy scattered hair with sleet-like ashes filled,

Thy breath congealed upon thy lips, thy cheeks
Fringed with a beard made white with other snows
Than those of age, thy forehead wrapped in clouds,
A leafless branch thy sceptre, and thy throne
A sliding car indebted to no wheels,
But urged by storms along its slippery way,
I love thee, all unlovely as thou seem'st,
And dreaded as thou art. Thou hold'st the sun
A prisoner in the yet undawning East,
Shortening his journey between morn and noon,
And hurrying him, impatient of his stay,
Down to the rosy west; but kindly still
Compensating his loss with added hours
Of social converse and instructive ease,
And gathering at short notice in one group
The family dispersed, and fixing thought
Not less dispersed by daylight and its cares.
I crown thee king of intimate delights,
Fire-side enjoyments, home-born happiness,
And all the comforts that the lowly roof
Of undisturbed retirement, and the hours
Of long uninterrupted evening know.
No rattling wheels stop short before these gates;
No powdered pert proficients in the art
Of sounding an alarm, assault these doors
Till the street rings; no stationary steeds
Cough their own knell, while heedless of the sound
The silent circle fan themselves, and quake:
But here the needle plies its busy task,
The pattern grows, the well-depicted flower,
Wrought patiently into the snowy lawn,
Unfolds its bosom; buds and leaves and sprigs
And curly tendrils, gracefully disposed,
Follow the nimble finger of the fair;
A wreath that cannot fade, of flowers that blow
With most success when all besides decay.
The poet's or historian's page, by one
Made vocal for the amusement of the rest;
The sprightly lyre, whose treasure of sweet sounds
The touch from many a trembling chord shakes out;
And the clear voice symphonious, yet distinct,
And in the charming strife triumphant still,
Beguile the night, and set a keener edge

On female industry; the threaded steel
Flies swiftly, and unfelt the task proceeds.
The volume closed, the customary rites
Of the last meal commence: a Roman meal,
Such as the mistress of the world once found
Delicious, when her patriots of high note,
Perhaps by moonlight, at their humble doors,
And under an old oak's domestic shade,
Enjoyed—spare feast!—a radish and an egg.
Discourse ensues, not trivial, yet not dull,
Nor such as with a frown forbids the play
Of fancy, or proscribes the sound of mirth;
Nor do we madly, like an impious world,
Who deem religion frenzy, and the God
That made them an intruder on their joys,
Start at His awful name, or deem His praise
A jarring note; themes of a graver tone
Exciting oft our gratitude and love,
While we retrace with memory's pointing wand
That calls the past to our exact review,
The dangers we have scaped, the broken snare,
The disappointed foe, deliverance found
Unlooked for, life preserved and peace restored,
Fruits of omnipotent eternal love:—
Oh evenings worthy of the gods! exclaimed
The Sabine bard. Oh evenings, I reply,
More to be prized and coveted than yours,
As more illumined and with nobler truths,
That I, and mine, and those we love, enjoy.

Is Winter hideous in a garb like this?
Needs he the tragic fur, the smoke of lamps,
The pent-up breath of an unsavoury throng
To thaw him into feeling, or the smart
And snappish dialogue that flippant wits
Call comedy, to prompt him with a smile?
The self-complacent actor, when he views
(Stealing a sidelong glance at a full house)
The slope of faces from the floor to the roof,
As if one master-spring controlled them all,
Relaxed into an universal grin,
Sees not a countenance there that speaks a joy
Half so refined or so sincere as ours.

Cards were superfluous here, with all the tricks
That idleness has ever yet contrived
To fill the void of an unfurnished brain,
To palliate dulness and give time a shove.
Time, as he passes us, has a dove's wing,
Unsoiled and swift and of a silken sound.
But the world's time is time in masquerade.
Theirs, should I paint him, has his pinions fledged
With motley plumes, and, where the peacock shows
His azure eyes, is tinctured black and red
With spots quadrangular of diamond form,
Ensanguined hearts, clubs typical of strife,
And spades, the emblem of untimely graves.
What should be, and what was an hour-glass once,
Becomes a dice-box, and a billiard mast
Well does the work of his destructive scythe.
Thus decked he charms a world whom fashion blinds
To his true worth, most pleased when idle most,
Whose only happy are their wasted hours.
Even misses, at whose age their mothers wore
The back-string and the bib, assume the dress
Of womanhood, sit pupils in the school
Of card-devoted time, and night by night,
Placed at some vacant corner of the board,
Learn every trick, and soon play all the game.
But truce with censure. Roving as I rove,
Where shall I find an end, or how proceed?
As he that travels far, oft turns aside
To view some rugged rock, or mouldering tower,
Which seen delights him not; then coming home,
Describes and prints it, that the world may know
How far he went for what was nothing worth;
So I, with brush in hand and pallet spread
With colours mixed for a far different use,
Paint cards and dolls, and every idle thing
That fancy finds in her excursive flights.

Come, Evening, once again, season of peace,
Return, sweet Evening, and continue long!
Methinks I see thee in the streaky west,
With matron-step slow moving, while the night
Treads on thy sweeping train; one hand employed
In letting fall the curtain of repose

On bird and beast, the other charged for man
With sweet oblivion of the cares of day;
Not sumptuously adorned, nor needing aid,
Like homely-featured night, of clustering gems,
A star or two just twinkling on thy brow
Suffices thee; save that the moon is thine
No less than hers, not worn indeed on high
With ostentatious pageantry, but set
With modest grandeur in thy purple zone,
Resplendent less, but of an ampler round.
Come, then, and thou shalt find thy votary calm,
Or make me so. Composure is thy gift;
And whether I devote thy gentle hours
To books, to music, or to poet's toil,
To weaving nets for bird-alluring fruit,
Or twining silken threads round ivory reels
When they command whom man was born to please,
I slight thee not, but make thee welcome still.

Just when our drawing-rooms begin to blaze
With lights, by clear reflection multiplied
From many a mirror, in which he of Gath,
Goliath, might have seen his giant bulk
Whole without stooping, towering crest and all,
My pleasures too begin. But me perhaps
The glowing hearth may satisfy a while
With faint illumination, that uplifts
The shadow to the ceiling, there by fits
Dancing uncouthly to the quivering flame.
Not undelightful is an hour to me
So spent in parlour twilight; such a gloom
Suits well the thoughtful or unthinking mind,
The mind contemplative, with some new theme
Pregnant, or indisposed alike to all.
Laugh ye, who boast your more mercurial powers
That never feel a stupor, know no pause,
Nor need one; I am conscious, and confess.
Fearless, a soul that does not always think.
Me oft has fancy ludicrous and wild
Soothed with a waking dream of houses, towers,
Trees, churches, and strange visages expressed
In the red cinders, while with poring eye
I gazed, myself creating what I saw.

Nor less amused have I quiescent watched
The sooty films that play upon the bars
Pendulous, and foreboding in the view
Of superstition, prophesying still,
Though still deceived, some stranger's near approach.
'Tis thus the understanding takes repose
In indolent vacuity of thought,
And sleeps and is refreshed. Meanwhile the face
Conceals the mood lethargic with a mask
Of deep deliberation, as the man
Were tasked to his full strength, absorbed and lost.
Thus oft reclined at ease, I lose an hour
At evening, till at length the freezing blast
That sweeps the bolted shutter, summons home
The recollected powers, and, snapping short
The glassy threads with which the fancy weaves
Her brittle toys, restores me to myself.
How calm is my recess! and how the frost
Raging abroad, and the rough wind, endear
The silence and the warmth enjoyed within!
I saw the woods and fields at close of day
A variegated show; the meadows green
Though faded, and the lands, where lately waved
The golden harvest, of a mellow brown,
Upturned so lately by the forceful share;
I saw far off the weedy fallows smile
With verdure not unprofitable, grazed
By flocks fast feeding, and selecting each
His favourite herb; while all the leafless groves
That skirt the horizon wore a sable hue,
Scarce noticed in the kindred dusk of eve.
To-morrow brings a change, a total change,
Which even now, though silently performed
And slowly, and by most unfelt, the face
Of universal nature undergoes.
Fast falls a fleecy shower; the downy flakes,
Descending and with never-ceasing lapse
Softly alighting upon all below,
Assimilate all objects. Earth receives
Gladly the thickening mantle, and the green
And tender blade, that feared the chilling blast,
Escapes unhurt beneath so warm a veil.

In such a world, so thorny, and where none
Finds happiness unblighted, or if found,
Without some thistly sorrow at its side,
It seems the part of wisdom, and no sin
Against the law of love, to measure lots
With less distinguished than ourselves, that thus
We may with patience bear our moderate ills,
And sympathise with others, suffering more.
Ill fares the traveller now, and he that stalks
In ponderous boots beside his reeking team;
The wain goes heavily, impeded sore
By congregating loads adhering close
To the clogged wheels, and, in its sluggish pace,
Noiseless appears a moving hill of snow.
The toiling steeds expand the nostril wide,
While every breath, by respiration strong
Forced downward, is consolidated soon
Upon their jutting chests. He, formed to bear
The pelting brunt of the tempestuous night,
With half-shut eyes, and puckered cheeks, and teeth
Presented bare against the storm, plods on;
One hand secures his hat, save when with both
He brandishes his pliant length of whip,
Resounding oft, and never heard in vain.
Oh happy, and, in my account, denied
That sensibility of pain with which
Refinement is endued, thrice happy thou!
Thy frame, robust and hardy, feels indeed
The piercing cold, but feels it unimpaired;
The learned finger never need explore
Thy vigorous pulse, and the unhealthful East,
That breathes the spleen, and searches every bone
Of the infirm, is wholesome air to thee.
Thy days roll on exempt from household care,
Thy waggon is thy wife; and the poor beasts,
That drag the dull companion to and fro,
Thine helpless charge, dependent on thy care.
Ah, treat them kindly! rude as thou appearest,
Yet show that thou hast mercy, which the great,
With needless hurry whirled from place to place,
Humane as they would seem, not always show.

Poor, yet industrious, modest, quiet, neat,

Such claim compassion in a night like this,
And have a friend in every feeling heart.
Warmed while it lasts, by labour, all day long
They brave the season, and yet find at eve,
Ill clad and fed but sparely, time to cool.
The frugal housewife trembles when she lights
Her scanty stock of brushwood, blazing clear,
But dying soon, like all terrestrial joys;
The few small embers left she nurses well.
And while her infant race with outspread hands
And crowded knees sit cowering o'er the sparks,
Retires, content to quake, so they be warmed.
The man feels least, as more inured than she
To winter, and the current in his veins
More briskly moved by his severer toil;
Yet he, too, finds his own distress in theirs.
The taper soon extinguished, which I saw
Dangled along at the cold finger's end
Just when the day declined, and the brown loaf
Lodged on the shelf, half-eaten, without sauce
Of sav'ry cheese, or butter costlier still,
Sleep seems their only refuge. For alas,
Where penury is felt the thought is chained,
And sweet colloquial pleasures are but few.
With all this thrift they thrive not. All the care
Ingenious parsimony takes, but just
Saves the small inventory, bed and stool,
Skillet and old carved chest, from public sale.
They live, and live without extorted alms
From grudging hands, but other boast have none
To soothe their honest pride that scorns to beg,
Nor comfort else, but in their mutual love.
I praise you much, ye meek and patient pair,
For ye are worthy; choosing rather far
A dry but independent crust, hard-earned
And eaten with a sigh, than to endure
The rugged frowns and insolent rebuffs
Of knaves in office, partial in their work
Of distribution; liberal of their aid
To clamorous importunity in rags,
But ofttimes deaf to suppliants who would blush
To wear a tattered garb however coarse,
Whom famine cannot reconcile to filth;

These ask with painful shyness, and, refused
Because deserving, silently retire.
But be ye of good courage! Time itself
Shall much befriend you. Time shall give increase,
And all your numerous progeny, well trained,
But helpless, in few years shall find their hands,
And labour too. Meanwhile ye shall not want
What, conscious of your virtues, we can spare,
Nor what a wealthier than ourselves may send.
I mean the man, who when the distant poor
Need help, denies them nothing but his name.

But poverty with most, who whimper forth
Their long complaints, is self-inflicted woe,
The effect of laziness or sottish waste.
Now goes the nightly thief prowling abroad
For plunder; much solicitous how best
He may compensate for a day of sloth,
By works of darkness and nocturnal wrong,
Woe to the gardener's pale, the farmer's hedge
Plashed neatly and secured with driven stakes
Deep in the loamy bank. Uptorn by strength
Resistless in so bad a cause, but lame
To better deeds, he bundles up the spoil—
An ass's burden,—and when laden most
And heaviest, light of foot steals fast away.
Nor does the boarded hovel better guard
The well-stacked pile of riven logs and roots
From his pernicious force. Nor will he leave
Unwrenched the door, however well secured,
Where chanticleer amidst his harem sleeps
In unsuspecting pomp; twitched from the perch
He gives the princely bird with all his wives
To his voracious bag, struggling in vain,
And loudly wondering at the sudden change.
Nor this to feed his own. 'Twere some excuse
Did pity of their sufferings warp aside
His principle, and tempt him into sin
For their support, so destitute; but they
Neglected pine at home, themselves, as more
Exposed than others, with less scruple made
His victims, robbed of their defenceless all.
Cruel is all he does. 'Tis quenchless thirst

Of ruinous ebriety that prompts
His every action, and imbrutes the man.
Oh for a law to noose the villain's neck
Who starves his own; who persecutes the blood
He gave them in his children's veins, and hates
And wrongs the woman he has sworn to love.

Pass where we may, through city, or through town,
Village or hamlet of this merry land,
Though lean and beggared, every twentieth pace
Conducts the unguarded nose to such a whiff
Of stale debauch, forth-issuing from the styes
That law has licensed, as makes temperance reel.
There sit involved and lost in curling clouds
Of Indian fume, and guzzling deep, the boor,
The lackey, and the groom. The craftsman there
Takes a Lethean leave of all his toil;
Smith, cobbler, joiner, he that plies the shears,
And he that kneads the dough: all loud alike,
All learned, and all drunk. The fiddle screams
Plaintive and piteous, as it wept and wailed
Its wasted tones and harmony unheard;
Fierce the dispute, whate'er the theme; while she,
Fell Discord, arbitress of such debate,
Perched on the sign-post, holds with even hand
Her undecisive scales. In this she lays
A weight of ignorance, in that, of pride,
And smiles delighted with the eternal poise.
Dire is the frequent curse and its twin sound
The cheek-distending oath, not to be praised
As ornamental, musical, polite,
Like those which modern senators employ,
Whose oath is rhetoric, and who swear for fame.
Behold the schools in which plebeian minds,
Once simple, are initiated in arts
Which some may practise with politer grace,
But none with readier skill! 'Tis here they learn
The road that leads from competence and peace
To indigence and rapine; till at last
Society, grown weary of the load,
Shakes her encumbered lap, and casts them out.
But censure profits little. Vain the attempt
To advertise in verse a public pest,

That, like the filth with which the peasant feeds
His hungry acres, stinks and is of use.
The excise is fattened with the rich result
Of all this riot; and ten thousand casks,
For ever dribbling out their base contents,
Touched by the Midas finger of the state,
Bleed gold for Ministers to sport away.
Drink and be mad then; 'tis your country bids!
Gloriously drunk, obey the important call,
Her cause demands the assistance of your throats;—
Ye all can swallow, and she asks no more.

Would I had fallen upon those happier days
That poets celebrate; those golden times
And those Arcadian scenes that Maro sings,
And Sidney, warbler of poetic prose.
Nymphs were Dianas then, and swains had hearts
That felt their virtues. Innocence, it seems,
From courts dismissed, found shelter in the groves;
The footsteps of simplicity, impressed
Upon the yielding herbage (so they sing),
Then were not all effaced. Then speech profane
And manners profligate were rarely found,
Observed as prodigies, and soon reclaimed.
Vain wish! those days were never: airy dreams
Sat for the picture; and the poet's hand,
Imparting substance to an empty shade,
Imposed a gay delirium for a truth.
Grant it: I still must envy them an age
That favoured such a dream, in days like these
Impossible, when virtue is so scarce
That to suppose a scene where she presides
Is tramontane, and stumbles all belief.
No. We are polished now. The rural lass,
Whom once her virgin modesty and grace,
Her artless manners and her neat attire,
So dignified, that she was hardly less
Than the fair shepherdess of old romance,
Is seen no more. The character is lost.
Her head adorned with lappets pinned aloft
And ribbons streaming gay, superbly raised
And magnified beyond all human size,
Indebted to some smart wig-weaver's hand

For more than half the tresses it sustains;
Her elbows ruffled, and her tottering form
Ill propped upon French heels; she might be deemed
(But that the basket dangling on her arm
Interprets her more truly) of a rank
Too proud for dairy-work, or sale of eggs;
Expect her soon with foot-boy at her heels,
No longer blushing for her awkward load,
Her train and her umbrella all her care.

The town has tinged the country; and the stain
Appears a spot upon a vestal's robe,
The worse for what it soils. The fashion runs
Down into scenes still rural, but alas,
Scenes rarely graced with rural manners now.
Time was when in the pastoral retreat
The unguarded door was safe; men did not watch
To invade another's right, or guard their own.
Then sleep was undisturbed by fear, unscared
By drunken howlings; and the chilling tale
Of midnight murder was a wonder heard
With doubtful credit, told to frighten babes
But farewell now to unsuspicious nights,
And slumbers unalarmed. Now, ere you sleep,
See that your polished arms be primed with care,
And drop the night-bolt. Ruffians are abroad,
And the first larum of the cock's shrill throat
May prove a trumpet, summoning your ear
To horrid sounds of hostile feet within.
Even daylight has its dangers; and the walk
Through pathless wastes and woods, unconscious once
Of other tenants than melodious birds,
Or harmless flocks, is hazardous and bold.
Lamented change! to which full many a cause
Inveterate, hopeless of a cure, conspires.
The course of human things from good to ill,
From ill to worse, is fatal, never fails.
Increase of power begets increase of wealth;
Wealth luxury, and luxury excess;
Excess, the scrofulous and itchy plague
That seizes first the opulent, descends
To the next rank contagious, and in time
Taints downward all the graduated scale

Of order, from the chariot to the plough.
The rich, and they that have an arm to check
The licence of the lowest in degree,
Desert their office; and themselves, intent
On pleasure, haunt the capital, and thus
To all the violence of lawless hands
Resign the scenes their presence might protect.
Authority itself not seldom sleeps,
Though resident, and witness of the wrong.
The plump convivial parson often bears
The magisterial sword in vain, and lays
His reverence and his worship both to rest
On the same cushion of habitual sloth.
Perhaps timidity restrains his arm,
When he should strike he trembles, and sets free,
Himself enslaved by terror of the band,
The audacious convict whom he dares not bind.
Perhaps, though by profession ghostly pure,
He, too, may have his vice, and sometimes prove
Less dainty than becomes his grave outside
In lucrative concerns. Examine well
His milk-white hand. The palm is hardly clean—
But here and there an ugly smutch appears.
Foh! 'twas a bribe that left it. He has touched
Corruption. Whoso seeks an audit here
Propitious, pays his tribute, game or fish,
Wildfowl or venison, and his errand speeds.

But faster far and more than all the rest
A noble cause, which none who bears a spark
Of public virtue ever wished removed,
Works the deplored and mischievous effect.
'Tis universal soldiership has stabbed
The heart of merit in the meaner class.
Arms, through the vanity and brainless rage
Of those that bear them, in whatever cause,
Seem most at variance with all moral good,
And incompatible with serious thought.
The clown, the child of nature, without guile,
Blest with an infant's ignorance of all
But his own simple pleasures, now and then
A wrestling match, a foot-race, or a fair,
Is balloted, and trembles at the news.

Sheepish he doffs his hat, and mumbling swears
A Bible-oath to be whate'er they please,
To do he knows not what. The task performed,
That instant he becomes the serjeant's care,
His pupil, and his torment, and his jest;
His awkward gait, his introverted toes,
Bent knees, round shoulders, and dejected looks,
Procure him many a curse. By slow degrees,
Unapt to learn and formed of stubborn stuff,
He yet by slow degrees puts off himself,
Grows conscious of a change, and likes it well.
He stands erect, his slouch becomes a walk,
He steps right onward, martial in his air,
His form and movement; is as smart above
As meal and larded locks can make him: wears
His hat or his plumed helmet with a grace,
And, his three years of heroship expired,
Returns indignant to the slighted plough.
He hates the field in which no fife or drum
Attends him, drives his cattle to a march,
And sighs for the smart comrades he has left.
'Twere well if his exterior change were all—
But with his clumsy port the wretch has lost
His ignorance and harmless manners too.
To swear, to game, to drink, to show at home
By lewdness, idleness, and Sabbath-breach,
The great proficiency he made abroad,
To astonish and to grieve his gazing friends,
To break some maiden's and his mother's heart,
To be a pest where he was useful once,
Are his sole aim, and all his glory now!
Man in society is like a flower
Blown in its native bed. 'Tis there alone
His faculties expanded in full bloom
Shine out, there only reach their proper use.
But man associated and leagued with man
By regal warrant, or self-joined by bond
For interest sake, or swarming into clans
Beneath one head for purposes of war,
Like flowers selected from the rest, and bound
And bundled close to fill some crowded vase,
Fades rapidly, and by compression marred
Contracts defilement not to be endured.

Hence chartered boroughs are such public plagues,
And burghers, men immaculate perhaps
In all their private functions, once combined,
Become a loathsome body, only fit
For dissolution, hurtful to the main.
Hence merchants, unimpeachable of sin
Against the charities of domestic life,
Incorporated, seem at once to lose
Their nature, and, disclaiming all regard
For mercy and the common rights of man,
Build factories with blood, conducting trade
At the sword's point, and dyeing the white robe
Of innocent commercial justice red.
Hence too the field of glory, as the world
Misdeems it, dazzled by its bright array,
With all the majesty of thundering pomp,
Enchanting music and immortal wreaths,
Is but a school where thoughtlessness is taught
On principle, where foppery atones
For folly, gallantry for every vice.

But slighted as it is, and by the great
Abandoned, and, which still I more regret,
Infected with the manners and the modes
It knew not once, the country wins me still.
I never framed a wish or formed a plan
That flattered me with hopes of earthly bliss,
But there I laid the scene. There early strayed
My fancy, ere yet liberty of choice
Had found me, or the hope of being free.
My very dreams were rural, rural too
The first-born efforts of my youthful muse,
Sportive, and jingling her poetic bells
Ere yet her ear was mistress of their powers.
No bard could please me but whose lyre was tuned
To Nature's praises. Heroes and their feats
Fatigued me, never weary of the pipe
Of Tityrus, assembling as he sang
The rustic throng beneath his favourite beech.
Then Milton had indeed a poet's charms:
New to my taste, his Paradise surpassed
The struggling efforts of my boyish tongue
To speak its excellence; I danced for joy.

I marvelled much that, at so ripe an age
As twice seven years, his beauties had then first
Engaged my wonder, and admiring still,
And still admiring, with regret supposed
The joy half lost because not sooner found.
Thee, too, enamoured of the life I loved,
Pathetic in its praise, in its pursuit
Determined, and possessing it at last
With transports such as favoured lovers feel,
I studied, prized, and wished that I had known,
Ingenious Cowley: and though now, reclaimed
By modern lights from an erroneous taste,
I cannot but lament thy splendid wit
Entangled in the cobwebs of the schools.
I still revere thee, courtly though retired,
Though stretched at ease in Chertsey's silent bowers,
Not unemployed, and finding rich amends
For a lost world in solitude and verse.
'Tis born with all. The love of Nature's works
Is an ingredient in the compound, man,
Infused at the creation of the kind.
And though the Almighty Maker has throughout
Discriminated each from each, by strokes
And touches of His hand, with so much art
Diversified, that two were never found
Twins at all points — yet this obtains in all,
That all discern a beauty in His works,
And all can taste them: minds that have been formed
And tutored, with a relish more exact,
But none without some relish, none unmoved.
It is a flame that dies not even there,
Where nothing feeds it. Neither business, crowds,
Nor habits of luxurious city life,
Whatever else they smother of true worth
In human bosoms, quench it or abate.
The villas, with which London stands begirt
Like a swarth Indian with his belt of beads,
Prove it. A breath of unadulterate air,
The glimpse of a green pasture, how they cheer
The citizen, and brace his languid frame!
Even in the stifling bosom of the town,
A garden in which nothing thrives, has charms
That soothe the rich possessor; much consoled

That here and there some sprigs of mournful mint,
Of nightshade, or valerian, grace the well
He cultivates. These serve him with a hint
That Nature lives; that sight-refreshing green
Is still the livery she delights to wear,
Though sickly samples of the exuberant whole.
What are the casements lined with creeping herbs,
The prouder sashes fronted with a range
Of orange, myrtle, or the fragrant weed,
The Frenchman's darling? are they not all proofs
That man, immured in cities, still retains
His inborn inextinguishable thirst
Of rural scenes, compensating his loss
By supplemental shifts, the best he may?
The most unfurnished with the means of life,
And they that never pass their brick-wall bounds
To range the fields, and treat their lungs with air,
Yet feel the burning instinct: over-head
Suspend their crazy boxes planted thick
And watered duly. There the pitcher stands
A fragment, and the spoutless tea-pot there;
Sad witnesses how close-pent man regrets
The country, with what ardour he contrives
A peep at nature, when he can no more.

Hail, therefore, patroness of health and ease
And contemplation, heart-consoling joys
And harmless pleasures, in the thronged abode
Of multitudes unknown, hail rural life!
Address himself who will to the pursuit
Of honours, or emolument, or fame,
I shall not add myself to such a chase,
Thwart his attempts, or envy his success.
Some must be great. Great offices will have
Great talents. And God gives to every man
The virtue, temper, understanding, taste,
That lifts him into life, and lets him fall
Just in the niche he was ordained to fill.
To the deliverer of an injured land
He gives a tongue to enlarge upon, a heart
To feel, and courage to redress her wrongs;
To monarchs dignity, to judges sense;
To artists ingenuity and skill;

To me an unambitious mind, content
In the low vale of life, that early felt
A wish for ease and leisure, and ere long
Found here that leisure and that ease I wished.

BOOK V.

THE WINTER MORNING WALK.

'Tis morning; and the sun, with ruddy orb
Ascending, fires the horizon; while the clouds,
That crowd away before the driving wind,
More ardent as the disk emerges more,
Resemble most some city in a blaze,
Seen through the leafless wood. His slanting ray
Slides ineffectual down the snowy vale,
And, tingeing all with his own rosy hue,
From every herb and every spiry blade
Stretches a length of shadow o'er the field,
Mine, spindling into longitude immense,
In spite of gravity, and sage remark
That I myself am but a fleeting shade,
Provokes me to a smile. With eye askance
I view the muscular proportioned limb
Transformed to a lean shank; the shapeless pair,
As they designed to mock me, at my side
Take step for step, and, as I near approach
The cottage, walk along the plastered wall,
Preposterous sight, the legs without the man.
The verdure of the plain lies buried deep
Beneath the dazzling deluge, and the bents
And coarser grass upspearing o'er the rest,
Of late unsightly and unseen, now shine
Conspicuous, and, in bright apparel clad,
And fledged with icy feathers, nod superb.
The cattle mourn in corners, where the fence
Screens them, and seem, half petrified, to sleep
In unrecumbent sadness. There they wait
Their wonted fodder, not, like hungering man,
Fretful if unsupplied, but silent, meek,
And patient of the slow-paced swain's delay.
He from the stack carves out the accustomed load,
Deep-plunging, and again deep-plunging oft
His broad keen knife into the solid mass:
Smooth as a wall the upright remnant stands,
With such undeviating and even force
He severs it away: no needless care,

81

Lest storms should overset the leaning pile
Deciduous, or its own unbalanced weight.
Forth goes the woodman, leaving unconcerned
The cheerful haunts of man, to wield the axe
And drive the wedge in yonder forest drear,
From morn to eve his solitary task.
Shaggy and lean and shrewd, with pointed ears
And tail cropped short, half lurcher and half cur,
His dog attends him. Close behind his heel
Now creeps he slow, and now with many a frisk,
Wide-scampering, snatches up the drifted snow
With ivory teeth, or ploughs it with his snout;
Then shakes his powdered coat and barks for joy.
Heedless of all his pranks the sturdy churl
Moves right toward the mark; nor stops for aught,
But now and then, with pressure of his thumb,
To adjust the fragrant charge of a short tube,
That fumes beneath his nose; the trailing cloud
Streams far behind him, scenting all the air.
Now from the roost, or from the neighbouring pale,
Where, diligent to catch the first faint gleam
Of smiling day, they gossiped side by side,
Come trooping at the housewife's well-known call
The feathered tribes domestic; half on wing,
And half on foot, they brush the fleecy flood,
Conscious, and fearful of too deep a plunge.
The sparrows peep, and quit the sheltering eaves
To seize the fair occasion; well they eye
The scattered grain, and, thievishly resolved
To escape the impending famine, often scared
As oft return, a pert, voracious kind.
Clean riddance quickly made, one only care
Remains to each, the search of sunny nook,
Or shed impervious to the blast. Resigned
To sad necessity the cock foregoes
His wonted strut, and, wading at their head
With well-considered steps, seems to resent
His altered gait, and stateliness retrenched.
How find the myriads, that in summer cheer
The hills and valleys with their ceaseless songs,
Due sustenance, or where subsist they now?
Earth yields them naught: the imprisoned worm is safe
Beneath the frozen clod; all seeds of herbs

Lie covered close, and berry-bearing thorns
That feed the thrush (whatever some suppose),
Afford the smaller minstrel no supply.
The long-protracted rigour of the year
Thins all their numerous flocks. In chinks and holes
Ten thousand seek an unmolested end,
As instinct prompts, self-buried ere they die.
The very rooks and daws forsake the fields,
Where neither grub nor root nor earth-nut now
Repays their labour more; and perched aloft
By the way-side, or stalking in the path,
Lean pensioners upon the traveller's track,
Pick up their nauseous dole, though sweet to them,
Of voided pulse, or half-digested grain.
The streams are lost amid the splendid blank,
O'erwhelming all distinction. On the flood
Indurated and fixed the snowy weight
Lies undissolved, while silently beneath
And unperceived the current steals away;
Not so where, scornful of a check, it leaps
The mill-dam, dashes on the restless wheel,
And wantons in the pebbly gulf below.
No frost can bind it there. Its utmost force
Can but arrest the light and smoky mist
That in its fall the liquid sheet throws wide.
And see where it has hung the embroidered banks
With forms so various, that no powers of art,
The pencil, or the pen, may trace the scene!
Here glittering turrets rise, upbearing high
(Fantastic misarrangement) on the roof
Large growth of what may seem the sparkling trees
And shrubs of fairy land. The crystal drops
That trickle down the branches, fast congealed,
Shoot into pillars of pellucid length
And prop the pile they but adorned before.
Here grotto within grotto safe defies
The sunbeam. There imbossed and fretted wild,
The growing wonder takes a thousand shapes
Capricious, in which fancy seeks in vain
The likeness of some object seen before.
Thus nature works as if to mock at art,
And in defiance of her rival powers;
By these fortuitous and random strokes

Performing such inimitable feats,
As she with all her rules can never reach.
Less worthy of applause though more admired,
Because a novelty, the work of man,
Imperial mistress of the fur-clad Russ,
Thy most magnificent and mighty freak,
The wonder of the North. No forest fell
When thou wouldst build; no quarry sent its stores
To enrich thy walls; but thou didst hew the floods,
And make thy marble of the glassy wave.
In such a palace Aristaeus found
Cyrene, when he bore the plaintive tale
Of his lost bees to her maternal ear.
In such a palace poetry might place
The armoury of winter, where his troops,
The gloomy clouds, find weapons, arrowy sleet,
Skin-piercing volley, blossom-bruising hail,
And snow that often blinds the traveller's course,
And wraps him in an unexpected tomb.
Silently as a dream the fabric rose.
No sound of hammer or of saw was there.
Ice upon ice, the well-adjusted parts
Were soon conjoined, nor other cement asked
Than water interfused to make them one.
Lamps gracefully disposed, and of all hues,
Illumined every side. A watery light
Gleamed through the clear transparency, that seemed
Another moon new-risen, or meteor fallen
From heaven to earth, of lambent flame serene.
So stood the brittle prodigy, though smooth
And slippery the materials, yet frost-bound
Firm as a rock. Nor wanted aught within
That royal residence might well befit,
For grandeur or for use. Long wavy wreaths
Of flowers, that feared no enemy but warmth,
Blushed on the panels. Mirror needed none
Where all was vitreous, but in order due
Convivial table and commodious seat
(What seemed at least commodious seat) were there,
Sofa and couch and high-built throne august.
The same lubricity was found in all,
And all was moist to the warm touch; a scene
Of evanescent glory, once a stream,

And soon to slide into a stream again.
Alas, 'twas but a mortifying stroke
Of undesigned severity, that glanced
(Made by a monarch) on her own estate,
On human grandeur and the courts of kings
'Twas transient in its nature, as in show
'Twas durable; as worthless, as it seemed
Intrinsically precious; to the foot
Treacherous and false; it smiled, and it was cold.

Great princes have great playthings. Some have played
At hewing mountains into men, and some
At building human wonders mountain high.
Some have amused the dull sad years of life
(Life spent in indolence, and therefore sad)
With schemes of monumental fame, and sought
By pyramids and mausoleum pomp,
Short-lived themselves, to immortalise their bones.
Some seek diversion in the tented field,
And make the sorrows of mankind their sport.
But war's a game which, were their subjects wise,
Kings should not play at. Nations would do well
To extort their truncheons from the puny hands
Of heroes whose infirm and baby minds
Are gratified with mischief, and who spoil,
Because men suffer it, their toy the world.

When Babel was confounded, and the great
Confederacy of projectors wild and vain
Was split into diversity of tongues,
Then, as a shepherd separates his flock,
These to the upland, to the valley those,
God drave asunder and assigned their lot
To all the nations. Ample was the boon
He gave them, in its distribution fair
And equal, and he bade them dwell in peace.
Peace was a while their care. They ploughed and sowed,
And reaped their plenty without grudge or strife,
But violence can never longer sleep
Than human passions please. In every heart
Are sown the sparks that kindle fiery war,
Occasion needs but fan them, and they blaze.
Cain had already shed a brother's blood:

The Deluge washed it out; but left unquenched
The seeds of murder in the breast of man.
Soon, by a righteous judgment, in the line
Of his descending progeny was found
The first artificer of death; the shrewd
Contriver who first sweated at the forge,
And forced the blunt and yet unblooded steel
To a keen edge, and made it bright for war.
Him Tubal named, the Vulcan of old times,
The sword and falchion their inventor claim,
And the first smith was the first murderer's son.
His art survived the waters; and ere long,
When man was multiplied and spread abroad
In tribes and clans, and had begun to call
These meadows and that range of hills his own,
The tasted sweets of property begat
Desire of more; and industry in some
To improve and cultivate their just demesne,
Made others covet what they saw so fair.
Thus wars began on earth. These fought for spoil,
And those in self-defence. Savage at first
The onset, and irregular. At length
One eminent above the rest, for strength,
For stratagem, or courage, or for all,
Was chosen leader. Him they served in war,
And him in peace for sake of warlike deeds
Reverenced no less. Who could with him compare?
Or who so worthy to control themselves
As he, whose prowess had subdued their foes?
Thus war, affording field for the display
Of virtue, made one chief, whom times of peace,
Which have their exigencies too, and call
For skill in government, at length made king.
King was a name too proud for man to wear
With modesty and meekness, and the crown,
So dazzling in their eyes who set it on,
Was sure to intoxicate the brows it bound.
It is the abject property of most,
That being parcel of the common mass,
And destitute of means to raise themselves,
They sink and settle lower than they need.
They know not what it is to feel within
A comprehensive faculty, that grasps

Great purposes with ease, that turns and wields,
Almost without an effort, plans too vast
For their conception, which they cannot move.
Conscious of impotence they soon grow drunk
With gazing, when they see an able man
Step forth to notice; and besotted thus
Build him a pedestal and say—Stand there,
And be our admiration and our praise.
They roll themselves before him in the dust,
Then most deserving in their own account
When most extravagant in his applause,
As if exalting him they raised themselves.
Thus by degrees, self-cheated of their sound
And sober judgment that he is but man,
They demi-deify and fume him so
That in due season he forgets it too.
Inflated and astrut with self-conceit
He gulps the windy diet, and ere long,
Adopting their mistake, profoundly thinks
The world was made in vain if not for him.
Thenceforth they are his cattle: drudges, born
To bear his burdens, drawing in his gears,
And sweating in his service. His caprice
Becomes the soul that animates them all.
He deems a thousand, or ten thousand lives,
Spent in the purchase of renown for him
An easy reckoning, and they think the same.
Thus kings were first invented, and thus kings
Were burnished into heroes, and became
The arbiters of this terraqueous swamp;
Storks among frogs, that have but croaked and died.
Strange that such folly, as lifts bloated man
To eminence fit only for a god,
Should ever drivel out of human lips,
Even in the cradled weakness of the world!
Still stranger much, that when at length mankind
Had reached the sinewy firmness of their youth,
And could discriminate and argue well
On subjects more mysterious, they were yet
Babes in the cause of freedom, and should fear
And quake before the gods themselves had made.
But above measure strange, that neither proof
Of sad experience, nor examples set

By some whose patriot virtue has prevailed,
Can even now, when they are grown mature
In wisdom, and with philosophic deeps
Familiar, serve to emancipate the rest!
Such dupes are men to custom, and so prone
To reverence what is ancient, and can plead
A course of long observance for its use,
That even servitude, the worst of ills,
Because delivered down from sire to son,
Is kept and guarded as a sacred thing.
But is it fit, or can it bear the shock
Of rational discussion, that a man,
Compounded and made up like other men
Of elements tumultuous, in whom lust
And folly in as ample measure meet,
As in the bosoms of the slaves he rules,
Should be a despot absolute, and boast
Himself the only freeman of his land?
Should when he pleases, and on whom he will,
Wage war, with any or with no pretence
Of provocation given, or wrong sustained,
And force the beggarly last doit, by means
That his own humour dictates, from the clutch
Of poverty, that thus he may procure
His thousands, weary of penurious life,
A splendid opportunity to die?
Say ye, who (with less prudence than of old
Jotham ascribed to his assembled trees
In politic convention) put your trust
I' th' shadow of a bramble, and recline
In fancied peace beneath his dangerous branch,
Rejoice in him and celebrate his sway,
Where find ye passive fortitude? Whence springs
Your self-denying zeal that holds it good
To stroke the prickly grievance, and to hang
His thorns with streamers of continual praise?
We too are friends to loyalty; we love
The king who loves the law, respects his bounds.
And reigns content within them; him we serve
Freely and with delight, who leaves us free;
But recollecting still that he is man,
We trust him not too far. King though he be,
And king in England, too, he may be weak

And vain enough to be ambitious still,
May exercise amiss his proper powers,
Or covet more than freemen choose to grant:
Beyond that mark is treason. He is ours,
To administer, to guard, to adorn the state,
But not to warp or change it. We are his,
To serve him nobly in the common cause
True to the death, but not to be his slaves.
Mark now the difference, ye that boast your love
Of kings, between your loyalty and ours.
We love the man; the paltry pageant you:
We the chief patron of the commonwealth;
You the regardless author of its woes:
We, for the sake of liberty, a king;
You chains and bondage for a tyrant's sake.

Our love is principle, and has its root
In reason, is judicious, manly, free;
Yours, a blind instinct, crouches to the rod,
And licks the foot that treads it in the dust.
Were kingship as true treasure as it seems,
Sterling, and worthy of a wise man's wish,
I would not be a king to be beloved
Causeless, and daubed with undiscerning praise,
Where love is more attachment to the throne,
Not to the man who fills it as he ought.

Whose freedom is by sufferance, and at will
Of a superior, he is never free.
Who lives, and is not weary of a life
Exposed to manacles, deserves them well.
The state that strives for liberty, though foiled
And forced to abandon what she bravely sought,
Deserves at least applause for her attempt,
And pity for her loss. But that's a cause
Not often unsuccessful; power usurped
Is weakness when opposed; conscious of wrong,
'Tis pusillanimous and prone to flight.
But slaves that once conceive the glowing thought
Of freedom, in that hope itself possess
All that the contest calls for; spirit, strength,
The scorn of danger, and united hearts,
The surest presage of the good they seek. *

The author hopes that he shall not be censured for unnecessary
warmth upon so interesting a subject. He is aware that it is become
almost fashionable to stigmatise such sentiments as no better than
empty declamation. But it is an ill symptom, and peculiar to modern
times. — C

Then shame to manhood, and opprobrious more
To France than all her losses and defeats,
Old or of later date, by sea or land,
Her house of bondage worse than that of old
Which God avenged on Pharaoh — the Bastille!
Ye horrid towers, the abode of broken hearts,
Ye dungeons and ye cages of despair,
That monarchs have supplied from age to age
With music such as suits their sovereign ears,
The sighs and groans of miserable men!
There's not an English heart that would not leap
To hear that ye were fallen at last, to know
That even our enemies, so oft employed
In forging chains for us, themselves were free.
For he that values liberty, confines
His zeal for her predominance within
No narrow bounds; her cause engages him
Wherever pleaded. 'Tis the cause of man.
There dwell the most forlorn of humankind,
Immured though unaccused, condemned untried,
Cruelly spared, and hopeless of escape.
There, like the visionary emblem seen
By him of Babylon, life stands a stump,
And filleted about with hoops of brass,
Still lives, though all its pleasant boughs are gone.
To count the hour bell and expect no change;
And ever as the sullen sound is heard,
Still to reflect that though a joyless note
To him whose moments all have one dull pace,
Ten thousand rovers in the world at large
Account it music; that it summons some
To theatre, or jocund feast, or ball;
The wearied hireling finds it a release
From labour, and the lover, that has chid
Its long delay, feels every welcome stroke
Upon his heart-strings trembling with delight; —
To fly for refuge from distracting thought

90

To such amusements as ingenious woe
Contrives, hard-shifting and without her tools;—
To read engraven on the mouldy walls,
In staggering types, his predecessor's tale,
A sad memorial, and subjoin his own;—
To turn purveyor to an overgorged
And bloated spider, till the pampered pest
Is made familiar, watches his approach,
Comes at his call, and serves him for a friend;—
To wear out time in numbering to and fro
The studs that thick emboss his iron door,
Then downward and then upward, then aslant
And then alternate, with a sickly hope
By dint of change to give his tasteless task
Some relish, till the sum, exactly found
In all directions, he begins again:—
Oh comfortless existence! hemmed around
With woes, which who that suffers would not kneel
And beg for exile, or the pangs of death?
That man should thus encroach on fellow-man,
Abridge him of his just and native rights,
Eradicate him, tear him from his hold
Upon the endearments of domestic life
And social, nip his fruitfulness and use,
And doom him for perhaps a heedless word
To barrenness and solitude and tears,
Moves indignation; makes the name of king
(Of king whom such prerogative can please)
As dreadful as the Manichean god,
Adored through fear, strong only to destroy.

'Tis liberty alone that gives the flower
Of fleeting life its lustre and perfume,
And we are weeds without it. All constraint,
Except what wisdom lays on evil men,
Is evil; hurts the faculties, impedes
Their progress in the road of science; blinds
The eyesight of discovery, and begets,
In those that suffer it, a sordid mind
Bestial, a meagre intellect, unfit
To be the tenant of man's noble form.
Thee therefore still, blameworthy as thou art,
With all thy loss of empire, and though squeezed

By public exigence, till annual food
Fails for the craving hunger of the state,
Thee I account still happy, and the chief
Among the nations, seeing thou art free,
My native nook of earth! Thy clime is rude,
Replete with vapours, and disposes much
All hearts to sadness, and none more than mine;
Thine unadulterate manners are less soft
And plausible than social life requires.
And thou hast need of discipline and art
To give thee what politer France receives
From Nature's bounty—that humane address
And sweetness, without which no pleasure is
In converse, either starved by cold reserve,
Or flushed with fierce dispute, a senseless brawl;
Yet, being free, I love thee; for the sake
Of that one feature, can be well content,
Disgraced as thou hast been, poor as thou art,
To seek no sublunary rest beside.
But once enslaved, farewell! I could endure
Chains nowhere patiently; and chains at home,
Where I am free by birthright, not at all.
Then what were left of roughness in the grain
Of British natures, wanting its excuse
That it belongs to freemen, would disgust
And shock me. I should then with double pain
Feel all the rigour of thy fickle clime;
And, if I must bewail the blessing lost
For which our Hampdens and our Sidneys bled,
I would at least bewail it under skies
Milder, among a people less austere,
In scenes which, having never known me free,
Would not reproach me with the loss I felt.
Do I forebode impossible events,
And tremble at vain dreams? Heaven grant I may,
But the age of virtuous politics is past,
And we are deep in that of cold pretence.
Patriots are grown too shrewd to be sincere,
And we too wise to trust them. He that takes
Deep in his soft credulity the stamp
Designed by loud declaimers on the part
Of liberty, themselves the slaves of lust,
Incurs derision for his easy faith

And lack of knowledge, and with cause enough.
For when was public virtue to be found,
Where private was not? Can he love the whole
Who loves no part? he be a nation's friend
Who is, in truth, the friend of no man there?
Can he be strenuous in his country's cause,
Who slights the charities for whose dear sake
That country, if at all, must be beloved?
— 'Tis therefore sober and good men are sad
For England's glory, seeing it wax pale
And sickly, while her champions wear their hearts
So loose to private duty, that no brain,
Healthful and undisturbed by factious fumes,
Can dream them trusty to the general weal.
Such were not they of old whose tempered blades
Dispersed the shackles of usurped control,
And hewed them link from link. Then Albion's sons
Were sons indeed. They felt a filial heart
Beat high within them at a mother's wrongs,
And shining each in his domestic sphere,
Shone brighter still once called to public view.
'Tis therefore many, whose sequestered lot
Forbids their interference, looking on,
Anticipate perforce some dire event;
And seeing the old castle of the state,
That promised once more firmness, so assailed
That all its tempest-beaten turrets shake,
Stand motionless expectants of its fall.
All has its date below. The fatal hour
Was registered in heaven ere time began.
We turn to dust, and all our mightiest works
Die too. The deep foundations that we lay,
Time ploughs them up, and not a trace remains.
We build with what we deem eternal rock;
A distant age asks where the fabric stood;
And in the dust, sifted and searched in vain,
The undiscoverable secret sleeps.

But there is yet a liberty unsung
By poets, and by senators unpraised,
Which monarchs cannot grant, nor all the power
Of earth and hell confederate take away;
A liberty, which persecution, fraud,

Oppression, prisons, have no power to bind,
Which whoso tastes can be enslaved no more:
'Tis liberty of heart, derived from heaven,
Bought with His blood who gave it to mankind,
And sealed with the same token. It is held
By charter, and that charter sanctioned sure
By the unimpeachable and awful oath
And promise of a God. His other gifts
All bear the royal stamp that speaks them His,
And are august, but this transcends them all.
His other works, this visible display
Of all-creating energy and might,
Are grand, no doubt, and worthy of the Word
That, finding an interminable space
Unoccupied, has filled the void so well,
And made so sparkling what was dark before.
But these are not His glory. Man, 'tis true,
Smit with the beauty of so fair a scene,
Might well suppose the Artificer Divine
Meant it eternal, had He not Himself
Pronounced it transient, glorious as it is,
And still designing a more glorious far,
Doomed it, as insufficient for His praise.
These, therefore, are occasional, and pass;
Formed for the confutation of the fool
Whose lying heart disputes against a God;
That office served, they must be swept away.
Not so the labours of His love; they shine
In other heavens than these that we behold,
And fade not. There is Paradise that fears
No forfeiture, and of its fruits He sends
Large prelibation oft to saints below.
Of these the first in order, and the pledge
And confident assurance of the rest,
Is liberty; a flight into His arms
Ere yet mortality's fine threads give way,
A clear escape from tyrannising lust,
And fill immunity from penal woe.

Chains are the portion of revolted man,
Stripes and a dungeon; and his body serves
The triple purpose. In that sickly, foul,
Opprobrious residence, he finds them all.

Propense his heart to idols, he is held
In silly dotage on created things
Careless of their Creator. And that low
And sordid gravitation of his powers
To a vile clod, so draws him with such force
Resistless from the centre he should seek,
That he at last forgets it. All his hopes
Tend downward, his ambition is to sink,
To reach a depth profounder still, and still
Profounder, in the fathomless abyss
Of folly, plunging in pursuit of death.
But ere he gain the comfortless repose
He seeks, and acquiescence of his soul,
In heaven renouncing exile, he endures
What does he not? from lusts opposed in vain,
And self-reproaching conscience. He foresees
The fatal issue to his health, fame, peace,
Fortune, and dignity; the loss of all
That can ennoble man, and make frail life,
Short as it is, supportable. Still worse,
Far worse than all the plagues with which his sins
Infect his happiest moments, he forebodes
Ages of hopeless misery; future death,
And death still future; not a hasty stroke,
Like that which sends him to the dusty grave,
But unrepealable enduring death.
Scripture is still a trumpet to his fears:
What none can prove a forgery, may be true;
What none but bad men wish exploded, must.
That scruple checks him. Riot is not loud
Nor drunk enough to drown it. In the midst
Of laughter his compunctions are sincere,
And he abhors the jest by which he shines.
Remorse begets reform. His master-lust
Falls first before his resolute rebuke,
And seems dethroned and vanquished. Peace ensues,
But spurious and short-lived, the puny child
Of self-congratulating Pride, begot
On fancied Innocence. Again he falls,
And fights again; but finds his best essay,
A presage ominous, portending still
Its own dishonour by a worse relapse,
Till Nature, unavailing Nature, foiled

So oft, and wearied in the vain attempt,
Scoffs at her own performance. Reason now
Takes part with appetite, and pleads the cause,
Perversely, which of late she so condemned;
With shallow shifts and old devices, worn
And tattered in the service of debauch,
Covering his shame from his offended sight.

"Hath God indeed given appetites to man,
And stored the earth so plenteously with means
To gratify the hunger of His wish,
And doth He reprobate and will He damn
The use of His own bounty? making first
So frail a kind, and then enacting laws
So strict, that less than perfect must despair?
Falsehood! which whoso but suspects of truth,
Dishonours God, and makes a slave of man.
Do they themselves, who undertake for hire
The teacher's office, and dispense at large
Their weekly dole of edifying strains,
Attend to their own music? have they faith
In what, with such solemnity of tone
And gesture, they propound to our belief?
Nay—conduct hath the loudest tongue. The voice
Is but an instrument on which the priest
May play what tune he pleases. In the deed,
The unequivocal authentic deed,
We find sound argument, we read the heart."

Such reasonings (if that name must needs belong
To excuses in which reason has no part)
Serve to compose a spirit well inclined
To live on terms of amity with vice,
And sin without disturbance. Often urged
(As often as, libidinous discourse
Exhausted, he resorts to solemn themes
Of theological and grave import),
They gain at last his unreserved assent,
Till, hardened his heart's temper in the forge
Of lust and on the anvil of despair,
He slights the strokes of conscience. Nothing moves,
Or nothing much, his constancy in ill;
Vain tampering has but fostered his disease,

'Tis desperate, and he sleeps the sleep of death.
Haste now, philosopher, and set him free.
Charm the deaf serpent wisely. Make him hear
Of rectitude and fitness: moral truth
How lovely, and the moral sense how sure,
Consulted and obeyed, to guide his steps
Directly to the FIRST AND ONLY FAIR.
Spare not in such a cause. Spend all the powers
Of rant and rhapsody in virtue's praise,
Be most sublimely good, verbosely grand,
And with poetic trappings grace thy prose
Till it outmantle all the pride of verse.—
Ah, tinkling cymbal and high-sounding brass
Smitten in vain! such music cannot charm
The eclipse that intercepts truth's heavenly beam,
And chills and darkens a wide-wandering soul.
The still small voice is wanted. He must speak,
Whose word leaps forth at once to its effect,
Who calls for things that are not, and they come.

Grace makes the slave a freeman. 'Tis a change
That turns to ridicule the turgid speech
And stately tone of moralists, who boast,
As if, like him of fabulous renown,
They had indeed ability to smooth
The shag of savage nature, and were each
An Orpheus and omnipotent in song.
But transformation of apostate man
From fool to wise, from earthly to divine,
Is work for Him that made him. He alone,
And He, by means in philosophic eyes
Trivial and worthy of disdain, achieves
The wonder; humanising what is brute
In the lost kind, extracting from the lips
Of asps their venom, overpowering strength
By weakness, and hostility by love.

Patriots have toiled, and in their country's cause
Bled nobly, and their deeds, as they deserve,
Receive proud recompense. We give in charge
Their names to the sweet lyre. The historic muse,
Proud of the treasure, marches with it down
To latest times; and sculpture, in her turn,

Gives bond in stone and ever-during brass,
To guard them, and to immortalise her trust.
But fairer wreaths are due, though never paid,
To those who, posted at the shrine of truth,
Have fallen in her defence. A patriot's blood
Well spent in such a strife may earn indeed,
And for a time ensure to his loved land,
The sweets of liberty and equal laws;
But martyrs struggle for a brighter prize,
And win it with more pain. Their blood is shed
In confirmation of the noblest claim,
Our claim to feed upon immortal truth,
To walk with God, to be divinely free,
To soar, and to anticipate the skies!
Yet few remember them. They lived unknown,
Till persecution dragged them into fame
And chased them up to heaven. Their ashes flew
—No marble tells us whither. With their names
No bard embalms and sanctifies his song,
And history, so warm on meaner themes,
Is cold on this. She execrates indeed
The tyranny that doomed them to the fire,
But gives the glorious sufferers little praise.

He is the freeman whom the truth makes free,
And all are slaves beside. There's not a chain
That hellish foes confederate for his harm
Can wind around him, but he casts it off
With as much ease as Samson his green withes.
He looks abroad into the varied field
Of Nature, and, though poor perhaps compared
With those whose mansions glitter in his sight,
Calls the delightful scenery all his own.
His are the mountains, and the valleys his,
And the resplendent river's. His to enjoy
With a propriety that none can feel,
But who, with filial confidence inspired,
Can lift to heaven an unpresumptuous eye,
And smiling say—My Father made them all!
Are they not his by a peculiar right,
And by an emphasis of interest his,
Whose eye they fill with tears of holy joy,
Whose heart with praise, and whose exalted mind

With worthy thoughts of that unwearied love
That planned, and built, and still upholds a world
So clothed with beauty, for rebellious man?
Yes—ye may fill your garners, ye that reap
The loaded soil, and ye may waste much good
In senseless riot; but ye will not find
In feast or in the chase, in song or dance,
A liberty like his, who, unimpeached
Of usurpation, and to no man's wrong,
Appropriates nature as his Father's work,
And has a richer use of yours, than you.
He is indeed a freeman. Free by birth
Of no mean city, planned or e'er the hills
Were built, the fountains opened, or the sea
With all his roaring multitude of waves.
His freedom is the same in every state;
And no condition of this changeful life
So manifold in cares, whose every day
Brings its own evil with it, makes it less.
For he has wings that neither sickness, pain,
Nor penury, can cripple or confine.
No nook so narrow but he spreads them there
With ease, and is at large. The oppressor holds
His body bound, but knows not what a range
His spirit takes, unconscious of a chain;
And that to bind him is a vain attempt,
Whom God delights in, and in whom He dwells.
Acquaint thyself with God if thou wouldst taste
His works. Admitted once to His embrace,
Thou shalt perceive that thou wast blind before;
Thine eye shall be instructed, and thine heart,
Made pure, shall relish, with divine delight
Till then unfelt, what hands divine have wrought.
Brutes graze the mountain-top with faces prone,
And eyes intent upon the scanty herb
It yields them; or, recumbent on its brow,
Ruminate, heedless of the scene outspread
Beneath, beyond, and stretching far away
From inland regions to the distant main.
Man views it and admires, but rests content
With what he views. The landscape has his praise,
But not its Author. Unconcerned who formed
The paradise he sees, he finds it such,

And such well pleased to find it, asks no more.
Not so the mind that has been touched from heaven,
And in the school of sacred wisdom taught
To read His wonders, in whose thought the world,
Fair as it is, existed ere it was.
Nor for its own sake merely, but for His
Much more who fashioned it, he gives it praise;
Praise that from earth resulting as it ought
To earth's acknowledged Sovereign, finds at once
Its only just proprietor in Him.
The soul that sees Him, or receives sublimed
New faculties or learns at least to employ
More worthily the powers she owned before;
Discerns in all things what, with stupid gaze
Of ignorance, till then she overlooked,
A ray of heavenly light gilding all forms
Terrestrial, in the vast and the minute
The unambiguous footsteps of the God
Who gives its lustre to an insect's wing
And wheels His throne upon the rolling worlds.
Much conversant with heaven, she often holds
With those fair ministers of light to man
That fill the skies nightly with silent pomp
Sweet conference; inquires what strains were they
With which heaven rang, when every star, in haste
To gratulate the new-created earth,
Sent forth a voice, and all the sons of God
Shouted for joy.—"Tell me, ye shining hosts
That navigate a sea that knows no storms,
Beneath a vault unsullied with a cloud,
If from your elevation, whence ye view
Distinctly scenes invisible to man
And systems of whose birth no tidings yet
Have reached this nether world, ye spy a race
Favoured as ours, transgressors from the womb
And hasting to a grave, yet doomed to rise
And to possess a brighter heaven than yours?
As one who, long detained on foreign shores,
Pants to return, and when he sees afar
His country's weather-bleached and battered rocks,
From the green wave emerging, darts an eye
Radiant with joy towards the happy land;
So I with animated hopes behold,

And many an aching wish, your beamy fires,
That show like beacons in the blue abyss,
Ordained to guide the embodied spirit home
From toilsome life to never-ending rest.
Love kindles as I gaze. I feel desires
That give assurance of their own success,
And that, infused from heaven, must thither tend."

So reads he Nature whom the lamp of truth
Illuminates. Thy lamp, mysterious Word!
Which whoso sees, no longer wanders lost
With intellect bemazed in endless doubt,
But runs the road of wisdom. Thou hast built,
With means that were not till by Thee employed,
Worlds that had never been, hadst Thou in strength
Been less, or less benevolent than strong.
They are Thy witnesses, who speak Thy power
And goodness infinite, but speak in ears
That hear not, or receive not their report.
In vain Thy creatures testify of Thee
Till Thou proclaim Thyself. Theirs is indeed
A teaching voice; but 'tis the praise of Thine
That whom it teaches it makes prompt to learn,
And with the boon gives talents for its use.
Till Thou art heard, imaginations vain
Possess the heart, and fables, false as hell,
Yet deemed oracular, lure down to death
The uninformed and heedless souls of men.
We give to chance, blind chance, ourselves as blind,
The glory of Thy work, which yet appears
Perfect and unimpeachable of blame,
Challenging human scrutiny, and proved
Then skilful most when most severely judged.
But chance is not; or is not where Thou reign'st:
Thy providence forbids that fickle power
(If power she be that works but to confound)
To mix her wild vagaries with Thy laws.
Yet thus we dote, refusing, while we can,
Instruction, and inventing to ourselves
Gods such as guilt makes welcome—gods that sleep,
Or disregard our follies, or that sit
Amused spectators of this bustling stage.
Thee we reject, unable to abide

Thy purity, till pure as Thou art pure,
Made such by Thee, we love Thee for that cause
For which we shunned and hated Thee before.
Then we are free: then liberty, like day,
Breaks on the soul, and by a flash from heaven
Fires all the faculties with glorious joy.
A voice is heard that mortal ears hear not
Till Thou hast touched them; 'tis the voice of song,
A loud Hosanna sent from all Thy works,
Which he that hears it with a shout repeats,
And adds his rapture to the general praise.
In that blest moment, Nature, throwing wide
Her veil opaque, discloses with a smile
The Author of her beauties, who, retired
Behind His own creation, works unseen
By the impure, and hears His power denied.
Thou art the source and centre of all minds,
Their only point of rest, eternal Word!
From Thee departing, they are lost and rove
At random, without honour, hope, or peace.
From Thee is all that soothes the life of man,
His high endeavour, and his glad success,
His strength to suffer, and his will to serve.
But, oh, Thou Bounteous Giver of all good,
Thou art of all Thy gifts Thyself the crown!
Give what Thou canst, without Thee we are poor,
And with Thee rich, take what Thou wilt away.

BOOK VI.

THE WINTER WALK AT NOON.

There is in souls a sympathy with sounds,
And as the mind is pitched the ear is pleased
With melting airs or martial, brisk or grave;
Some chord in unison with what we hear
Is touched within us, and the heart replies.
How soft the music of those village bells
Falling at intervals upon the ear
In cadence sweet, now dying all away,
Now pealing loud again, and louder still,
Clear and sonorous as the gale comes on.
With easy force it opens all the cells
Where memory slept. Wherever I have heard
A kindred melody, the scene recurs,
And with it all its pleasures and its pains.
Such comprehensive views the spirit takes,
That in a few short moments I retrace
(As in a map the voyager his course)
The windings of my way through many years.
Short as in retrospect the journey seems,
It seemed not always short; the rugged path,
And prospect oft so dreary and forlorn,
Moved many a sigh at its disheartening length.
Yet feeling present evils, while the past
Faintly impress the mind, or not at all,
How readily we wish time spent revoked,
That we might try the ground again, where once
(Through inexperience as we now perceive)
We missed that happiness we might have found.
Some friend is gone, perhaps his son's best friend
A father, whose authority, in show
When most severe, and mustering all its force,
Was but the graver countenance of love;
Whose favour, like the clouds of spring, might lower,
And utter now and then an awful voice,
But had a blessing in its darkest frown,
Threatening at once and nourishing the plant.
We loved, but not enough, the gentle hand
That reared us. At a thoughtless age allured

By every gilded folly, we renounced
His sheltering side, and wilfully forewent
That converse which we now in vain regret.
How gladly would the man recall to life
The boy's neglected sire! a mother too,
That softer friend, perhaps more gladly still,
Might he demand them at the gates of death.
Sorrow has since they went subdued and tamed
The playful humour; he could now endure
(Himself grown sober in the vale of tears)
And feel a parent's presence no restraint.
But not to understand a treasure's worth
Till time has stolen away the slighted good,
Is cause of half the poverty we feel,
And makes the world the wilderness it is.
The few that pray at all, pray oft amiss,
And, seeking grace to improve the prize they hold,
Would urge a wiser suit than asking more.

The night was winter in his roughest mood,
The morning sharp and clear; but now at noon
Upon the southern side of the slant hills,
And where the woods fence off the northern blast,
The season smiles, resigning all its rage,
And has the warmth of May. The vault is blue
Without a cloud, and white without a speck
The dazzling splendour of the scene below.
Again the harmony comes o'er the vale,
And through the trees I view the embattled tower
Whence all the music. I again perceive
The soothing influence of the wafted strains,
And settle in soft musings, as I tread
The walk still verdant under oaks and elms,
Whose outspread branches overarch the glade.
The roof, though movable through all its length,
As the wind sways it, has yet well sufficed,
And, intercepting in their silent fall
The frequent flakes, has kept a path for me.
No noise is here, or none that hinders thought:
The redbreast warbles still, but is content
With slender notes and more than half suppressed.
Pleased with his solitude, and flitting light
From spray to spray, where'er he rests he shakes

From many a twig the pendant drops of ice,
That tinkle in the withered leaves below.
Stillness, accompanied with sounds so soft,
Charms more than silence. Meditation here
May think down hours to moments. Here the heart
May give an useful lesson to the head,
And learning wiser grow without his books.
Knowledge and wisdom, far from being one,
Have ofttimes no connection. Knowledge dwells
In heads replete with thoughts of other men;
Wisdom in minds attentive to their own.
Knowledge, a rude unprofitable mass,
The mere materials with which wisdom builds,
Till smoothed and squared and fitted to its place,
Does but encumber whom it seems to enrich.
Knowledge is proud that he has learned so much,
Wisdom is humble that he knows no more.
Books are not seldom talismans and spells
By which the magic art of shrewder wits
Holds an unthinking multitude enthralled.
Some to the fascination of a name
Surrender judgment hoodwinked. Some the style
Infatuates, and, through labyrinths and wilds
Of error, leads them by a tune entranced.
While sloth seduces more, too weak to bear
The insupportable fatigue of thought,
And swallowing therefore without pause or choice
The total grist unsifted, husks and all.
But trees, and rivulets whose rapid course
Defies the check of winter, haunts of deer,
And sheep-walks populous with bleating lambs,
And lanes, in which the primrose ere her time
Peeps through the moss that clothes the hawthorn root,
Deceive no student. Wisdom there, and truth,
Not shy as in the world, and to be won
By slow solicitation, seize at once
The roving thought, and fix it on themselves.

What prodigies can power divine perform
More grand than it produces year by year,
And all in sight of inattentive man?
Familiar with the effect we slight the cause,
And in the constancy of Nature's course,

The regular return of genial months,
And renovation of a faded world,
See nought to wonder at. Should God again,
As once in Gibeon, interrupt the race
Of the undeviating and punctual sun,
How would the world admire! but speaks it less
An agency divine, to make him know
His moment when to sink and when to rise
Age after age, than to arrest his course?
All we behold is miracle: but, seen
So duly, all is miracle in vain.
Where now the vital energy that moved,
While summer was, the pure and subtle lymph
Through the imperceptible meandering veins
Of leaf and flower? It sleeps: and the icy touch
Of unprolific winter has impressed
A cold stagnation on the intestine tide.
But let the months go round, a few short months,
And all shall be restored. These naked shoots,
Barren as lances, among which the wind
Makes wintry music, sighing as it goes,
Shall put their graceful foliage on again,
And more aspiring and with ampler spread
Shall boast new charms, and more than they have lost.
Then, each in its peculiar honours clad,
Shall publish even to the distant eye
Its family and tribe. Laburnum rich
In streaming gold; syringa ivory pure;
The scented and the scentless rose; this red
And of a humbler growth, the other tall,
And throwing up into the darkest gloom
Of neighbouring cypress, or more sable yew,
Her silver globes, light as the foamy surf
That the wind severs from the broken wave;
The lilac various in array, now white,
Now sanguine, and her beauteous head now set
With purple spikes pyramidal, as if
Studious of ornament, yet unresolved
Which hue she most approved, she chose them all;
Copious of flowers the woodbine, pale and wan,
But well compensating their sickly looks
With never-cloying odours, early and late;
Hypericum all bloom, so thick a swarm

Of flowers like flies, clothing her slender rods,
That scarce a leaf appears; mezereon too,
Though leafless, well attired, and thick beset
With blushing wreaths investing every spray;
Althaea with the purple eye; the broom,
Yellow and bright as bullion unalloyed
Her blossoms; and luxuriant above all
The jasmine, throwing wide her elegant sweets,
The deep dark green of whose unvarnished leaf
Makes more conspicuous, and illumines more
The bright profusion of her scattered stars. —
These have been, and these shall be in their day,
And all this uniform uncoloured scene
Shall be dismantled of its fleecy load,
And flush into variety again.
From dearth to plenty, and from death to life,
Is Nature's progress when she lectures man
In heavenly truth; evincing, as she makes
The grand transition, that there lives and works
A soul in all things, and that soul is God.
The beauties of the wilderness are His,
That make so gay the solitary place
Where no eye sees them. And the fairer forms
That cultivation glories in, are His.
He sets the bright procession on its way,
And marshals all the order of the year.
He marks the bounds which Winter may not pass,
And blunts his pointed fury. In its case,
Russet and rude, folds up the tender germ
Uninjured, with inimitable art,
And, ere one flowery season fades and dies,
Designs the blooming wonders of the next.

Some say that in the origin of things,
When all creation started into birth,
The infant elements received a law
From which they swerve not since; that under force
Of that controlling ordinance they move,
And need not His immediate hand, who first
Prescribed their course, to regulate it now.
Thus dream they, and contrive to save a God
The encumbrance of His own concerns, and spare
The great Artificer of all that moves

The stress of a continual act, the pain
Of unremitted vigilance and care,
As too laborious and severe a task.
So man the moth is not afraid, it seems,
To span Omnipotence, and measure might
That knows no measure, by the scanty rule
And standard of his own, that is to-day,
And is not ere to-morrow's sun go down.
But how should matter occupy a charge
Dull as it is, and satisfy a law
So vast in its demands, unless impelled
To ceaseless service by a ceaseless force,
And under pressure of some conscious cause?
The Lord of all, Himself through all diffused
Sustains and is the life of all that lives.
Nature is but a name for an effect
Whose cause is God. He feeds the secret fire
By which the mighty process is maintained,
Who sleeps not, is not weary; in whose sight
Slow-circling ages are as transient days;
Whose work is without labour, whose designs
No flaw deforms, no difficulty thwarts,
And whose beneficence no charge exhausts.
Him blind antiquity profaned, not served,
With self-taught rites and under various names
Female and male, Pomona, Pales, Pan,
And Flora and Vertumnus; peopling earth
With tutelary goddesses and gods
That were not, and commending as they would
To each some province, garden, field, or grove.
But all are under One. One spirit—His
Who bore the platted thorns with bleeding brows—
Rules universal nature. Not a flower
But shows some touch in freckle, streak, or stain,
Of His unrivalled pencil. He inspires
Their balmy odours and imparts their hues,
And bathes their eyes with nectar, and includes,
In grains as countless as the sea-side sands,
The forms with which He sprinkles all the earth.
Happy who walks with Him! whom, what he finds
Of flavour or of scent in fruit or flower,
Or what he views of beautiful or grand
In nature, from the broad majestic oak

To the green blade that twinkles in the sun,
Prompts with remembrance of a present God.
His presence, who made all so fair, perceived,
Makes all still fairer. As with Him no scene
Is dreary, so with Him all seasons please.
Though winter had been none had man been true,
And earth be punished for its tenant's sake,
Yet not in vengeance; as this smiling sky,
So soon succeeding such an angry night,
And these dissolving snows, and this clear stream,
Recovering fast its liquid music, prove.

Who then, that has a mind well strung and tuned
To contemplation, and within his reach
A scene so friendly to his favourite task,
Would waste attention at the chequered board,
His host of wooden warriors to and fro
Marching and counter-marching, with an eye
As fixt as marble, with a forehead ridged
And furrowed into storms, and with a hand
Trembling, as if eternity were hung
In balance on his conduct of a pin?
Nor envies he aught more their idle sport,
Who pant with application misapplied
To trivial toys, and, pushing ivory balls
Across the velvet level, feel a joy
Akin to rapture, when the bauble finds
Its destined goal of difficult access.
Nor deems he wiser him, who gives his noon
To Miss, the Mercer's plague, from shop to shop
Wandering, and littering with unfolded silks
The polished counter, and approving none,
Or promising with smiles to call again.
Nor him, who, by his vanity seduced,
And soothed into a dream that he discerns
The difference of a Guido from a daub,
Frequents the crowded auction. Stationed there
As duly as the Langford of the show,
With glass at eye, and catalogue in hand,
And tongue accomplished in the fulsome cant
And pedantry that coxcombs learn with ease,
Oft as the price-deciding hammer falls
He notes it in his book, then raps his box,

Swears 'tis a bargain, rails at his hard fate
That he has let it pass—but never bids.

Here unmolested, through whatever sign
The sun proceeds, I wander; neither mist,
Nor freezing sky, nor sultry, checking me,
Nor stranger intermeddling with my joy.
Even in the spring and play-time of the year
That calls the unwonted villager abroad
With all her little ones, a sportive train,
To gather king-cups in the yellow mead,
And prank their hair with daisies, or to pick
A cheap but wholesome salad from the brook,
These shades are all my own. The timorous hare,
Grown so familiar with her frequent guest,
Scarce shuns me; and the stock-dove unalarmed
Sits cooing in the pine-tree, nor suspends
His long love-ditty for my near approach.
Drawn from his refuge in some lonely elm
That age or injury has hollowed deep,
Where on his bed of wool and matted leaves
He has outslept the winter, ventures forth
To frisk awhile, and bask in the warm sun,
The squirrel, flippant, pert, and full of play.
He sees me, and at once, swift as a bird,
Ascends the neighbouring beech; there whisks his brush,
And perks his ears, and stamps and scolds aloud,
With all the prettiness of feigned alarm,
And anger insignificantly fierce.

The heart is hard in nature, and unfit
For human fellowship, as being void
Of sympathy, and therefore dead alike
To love and friendship both, that is not pleased
With sight of animals enjoying life,
Nor feels their happiness augment his own.
The bounding fawn that darts across the glade
When none pursues, through mere delight of heart,
And spirits buoyant with excess of glee;
The horse, as wanton and almost as fleet,
That skims the spacious meadow at full speed,
Then stops and snorts, and throwing high his heels
Starts to the voluntary race again;

The very kine that gambol at high noon,
The total herd receiving first from one,
That leads the dance, a summons to be gay,
Though wild their strange vagaries, and uncouth
Their efforts, yet resolved with one consent
To give such act and utterance as they may
To ecstasy too big to be suppressed —
These, and a thousand images of bliss,
With which kind nature graces every scene
Where cruel man defeats not her design,
Impart to the benevolent, who wish
All that are capable of pleasure pleased,
A far superior happiness to theirs,
The comfort of a reasonable joy.

Man scarce had risen, obedient to His call
Who formed him from the dust, his future grave,
When he was crowned as never king was since.
God set His diadem upon his head,
And angel choirs attended. Wondering stood
The new-made monarch, while before him passed,
All happy and all perfect in their kind,
The creatures, summoned from their various haunts
To see their sovereign, and confess his sway.
Vast was his empire, absolute his power,
Or bounded only by a law whose force
'Twas his sublimest privilege to feel
And own, the law of universal love.
He ruled with meekness, they obeyed with joy.
No cruel purpose lurked within his heart,
And no distrust of his intent in theirs.
So Eden was a scene of harmless sport,
Where kindness on his part who ruled the whole
Begat a tranquil confidence in all,
And fear as yet was not, nor cause for fear.
But sin marred all; and the revolt of man,
That source of evils not exhausted yet,
Was punished with revolt of his from him.
Garden of God, how terrible the change
Thy groves and lawns then witnessed! every heart,
Each animal of every name, conceived
A jealousy and an instinctive fear,
And, conscious of some danger, either fled

Precipitate the loathed abode of man,
Or growled defiance in such angry sort,
As taught him too to tremble in his turn.
Thus harmony and family accord
Were driven from Paradise; and in that hour
The seeds of cruelty, that since have swelled
To such gigantic and enormous growth,
Were sown in human nature's fruitful soil.
Hence date the persecution and the pain
That man inflicts on all inferior kinds,
Regardless of their plaints. To make him sport,
To gratify the frenzy of his wrath,
Or his base gluttony, are causes good
And just in his account, why bird and beast
Should suffer torture, and the streams be dyed
With blood of their inhabitants impaled.
Earth groans beneath the burden of a war
Waged with defenceless innocence, while he,
Not satisfied to prey on all around,
Adds tenfold bitterness to death by pangs
Needless, and first torments ere he devours.
Now happiest they that occupy the scenes
The most remote from his abhorred resort,
Whom once as delegate of God on earth
They feared, and as His perfect image loved.
The wilderness is theirs with all its caves,
Its hollow glens, its thickets, and its plains
Unvisited by man. There they are free,
And howl and roar as likes them, uncontrolled,
Nor ask his leave to slumber or to play.
Woe to the tyrant, if he dare intrude
Within the confines of their wild domain;
The lion tells him, "I am monarch here;"
And if he spares him, spares him on the terms
Of royal mercy, and through generous scorn
To rend a victim trembling at his foot.
In measure, as by force of instinct drawn,
Or by necessity constrained, they live
Dependent upon man, those in his fields,
These at his crib, and some beneath his roof;
They prove too often at how dear a rate
He sells protection. Witness, at his foot
The spaniel dying for some venial fault,

Under dissection of the knotted scourge;
Witness the patient ox, with stripes and yells
Driven to the slaughter, goaded as he runs
To madness, while the savage at his heels
Laughs at the frantic sufferer's fury spent
Upon the guiltless passenger o'erthrown.
He too is witness, noblest of the train
That wait on man, the flight-performing horse:
With unsuspecting readiness he takes
His murderer on his back, and, pushed all day,
With bleeding sides, and flanks that heave for life,
To the far-distant goal, arrives and dies.
So little mercy shows who needs so much!
Does law, so jealous in the cause of man,
Denounce no doom on the delinquent? None.
He lives, and o'er his brimming beaker boasts
(As if barbarity were high desert)
The inglorious feat, and, clamorous in praise
Of the poor brute, seems wisely to suppose
The honours of his matchless horse his own.
But many a crime, deemed innocent on earth,
Is registered in heaven, and these, no doubt,
Have each their record, with a curse annexed.
Man may dismiss compassion from his heart,
But God will never. When He charged the Jew
To assist his foe's down-fallen beast to rise,
And when the bush-exploring boy that seized
The young, to let the parent bird go free,
Proved He not plainly that His meaner works
Are yet His care, and have an interest all,
All, in the universal Father's love?
On Noah, and in him on all mankind,
The charter was conferred by which we hold
The flesh of animals in fee, and claim,
O'er all we feed on, power of life and death.
But read the instrument, and mark it well;
The oppression of a tyrannous control
Can find no warrant there. Feed then, and yield
Thanks for thy food. Carnivorous, through sin,
Feed on the slain, but spare the living brute.

The Governor of all, Himself to all
So bountiful, in whose attentive ear

The unfledged raven and the lion's whelp
Plead not in vain for pity on the pangs
Of hunger unassuaged, has interposed,
Not seldom, His avenging arm, to smite
The injurious trampler upon nature's law,
That claims forbearance even for a brute.
He hates the hardness of a Balaam's heart,
And, prophet as he was, he might not strike
The blameless animal, without rebuke,
On which he rode. Her opportune offence
Saved him, or the unrelenting seer had died.
He sees that human equity is slack
To interfere, though in so just a cause,
And makes the task His own; inspiring dumb
And helpless victims with a sense so keen
Of injury, with such knowledge of their strength,
And such sagacity to take revenge,
That oft the beast has seemed to judge the man.
An ancient, not a legendary tale,
By one of sound intelligence rehearsed,
(If such, who plead for Providence may seem
In modern eyes) shall make the doctrine clear.

Where England, stretched towards the setting sun,
Narrow and long, o'erlooks the western wave,
Dwelt young Misagathus; a scorner he
Of God and goodness, atheist in ostent,
Vicious in act, in temper savage-fierce.
He journeyed, and his chance was, as he went,
To join a traveller of far different note —
Evander, famed for piety, for years
Deserving honour, but for wisdom more.
Fame had not left the venerable man
A stranger to the manners of the youth,
Whose face, too, was familiar to his view.
Their way was on the margin of the land,
O'er the green summit of the rocks whose base
Beats back the roaring surge, scarce heard so high.
The charity that warmed his heart was moved
At sight of the man-monster. With a smile
Gentle and affable, and full of grace,
As fearful of offending whom he wished
Much to persuade, he plied his ear with truths

Not harshly thundered forth or rudely pressed,
But, like his purpose, gracious, kind, and sweet.
"And dost thou dream," the impenetrable man
Exclaimed, "that me the lullabies of age,
And fantasies of dotards such as thou,
Can cheat, or move a moment's fear in me?
Mark now the proof I give thee, that the brave
Need no such aids as superstition lends
To steel their hearts against the dread of death."
He spoke, and to the precipice at hand
Pushed with a madman's fury. Fancy shrinks,
And the blood thrills and curdles at the thought
Of such a gulf as he designed his grave.
But though the felon on his back could dare
The dreadful leap, more rational, his steed
Declined the death, and wheeling swiftly round,
Or ere his hoof had pressed the crumbling verge,
Baffled his rider, saved against his will.
The frenzy of the brain may be redressed
By medicine well applied, but without grace
The heart's insanity admits no cure.
Enraged the more by what might have reformed
His horrible intent, again he sought
Destruction, with a zeal to be destroyed,
With sounding whip and rowels dyed in blood.
But still in vain. The Providence that meant
A longer date to the far nobler beast,
Spared yet again the ignobler for his sake.
And now, his prowess proved, and his sincere,
Incurable obduracy evinced,
His rage grew cool; and, pleased perhaps to have earned
So cheaply the renown of that attempt,
With looks of some complacence he resumed
His road, deriding much the blank amaze
Of good Evander, still where he was left
Fixed motionless, and petrified with dread.
So on they fared; discourse on other themes
Ensuing, seemed to obliterate the past,
And tamer far for so much fury shown
(As is the course of rash and fiery men)
The rude companion smiled as if transformed.
But 'twas a transient calm. A storm was near,
An unsuspected storm. His hour was come.

The impious challenger of power divine
Was now to learn that Heaven, though slow to wrath,
Is never with impunity defied.
His horse, as he had caught his master's mood,
Snorting, and starting into sudden rage,
Unbidden, and not now to be controlled,
Rushed to the cliff, and having reached it, stood.
At once the shock unseated him; he flew
Sheer o'er the craggy barrier, and, immersed
Deep in the flood, found, when he sought it not,
The death he had deserved, and died alone.
So God wrought double justice; made the fool
The victim of his own tremendous choice,
And taught a brute the way to safe revenge.

I would not enter on my list of friends
(Though graced with polished manners and fine sense,
Yet wanting sensibility) the man
Who needlessly sets foot upon a worm.
An inadvertent step may crush the snail
That crawls at evening in the public path;
But he that has humanity, forewarned,
Will tread aside, and let the reptile live.
The creeping vermin, loathsome to the sight,
And charged perhaps with venom, that intrudes
A visitor unwelcome into scenes
Sacred to neatness and repose, the alcove,
The chamber, or refectory, may die.
A necessary act incurs no blame.
Not so when, held within their proper bounds
And guiltless of offence, they range the air,
Or take their pastime in the spacious field.
There they are privileged; and he that hunts
Or harms them there is guilty of a wrong,
Disturbs the economy of Nature's realm,
Who, when she formed, designed them an abode.
The sum is this: if man's convenience, health,
Or safety interfere, his rights and claims
Are paramount, and must extinguish theirs.
Else they are all—the meanest things that are—
As free to live and to enjoy that life,
As God was free to form them at the first,
Who in His sovereign wisdom made them all.

Ye, therefore, who love mercy, teach your sons
To love it too. The spring-time of our years
Is soon dishonoured and defiled in most
By budding ills, that ask a prudent hand
To check them. But, alas! none sooner shoots,
If unrestrained, into luxuriant growth,
Than cruelty, most devilish of them all.
Mercy to him that shows it, is the rule
And righteous limitation of its act,
By which Heaven moves in pardoning guilty man;
And he that shows none, being ripe in years,
And conscious of the outrage he commits,
Shall seek it and not find it in his turn.

Distinguished much by reason, and still more
By our capacity of grace divine,
From creatures that exist but for our sake,
Which having served us, perish, we are held
Accountable, and God, some future day,
Will reckon with us roundly for the abuse
Of what He deems no mean or trivial trust.
Superior as we are, they yet depend
Not more on human help, than we on theirs.
Their strength, or speed, or vigilance, were given
In aid of our defects. In some are found
Such teachable and apprehensive parts,
That man's attainments in his own concerns,
Matched with the expertness of the brutes in theirs,
Are ofttimes vanquished and thrown far behind.
Some show that nice sagacity of smell,
And read with such discernment, in the port
And figure of the man, his secret aim,
That oft we owe our safety to a skill
We could not teach, and must despair to learn.
But learn we might, if not too proud to stoop
To quadruped instructors, many a good
And useful quality, and virtue too,
Rarely exemplified among ourselves;
Attachment never to be weaned, or changed
By any change of fortune, proof alike
Against unkindness, absence, and neglect;
Fidelity, that neither bribe nor threat
Can move or warp; and gratitude for small

And trivial favours, lasting as the life,
And glistening even in the dying eye.

Man praises man. Desert in arts or arms
Wins public honour; and ten thousand sit
Patiently present at a sacred song,
Commemoration-mad; content to hear
(Oh wonderful effect of music's power!)
Messiah's eulogy, for Handel's sake.
But less, methinks, than sacrilege might serve—
(For was it less? What heathen would have dared
To strip Jove's statue of his oaken wreath
And hang it up in honour of a man?)
Much less might serve, when all that we design
Is but to gratify an itching ear,
And give the day to a musician's praise.
Remember Handel! who, that was not born
Deaf as the dead to harmony, forgets,
Or can, the more than Homer of his age?
Yes—we remember him; and, while we praise
A talent so divine, remember too
That His most holy Book from whom it came
Was never meant, was never used before
To buckram out the memory of a man.
But hush!—the muse perhaps is too severe,
And with a gravity beyond the size
And measure of the offence, rebukes a deed
Less impious than absurd, and owing more
To want of judgment than to wrong design.
So in the chapel of old Ely House,
When wandering Charles, who meant to be the third,
Had fled from William, and the news was fresh,
The simple clerk, but loyal, did announce,
And eke did rear right merrily, two staves,
Sung to the praise and glory of King George.
—Man praises man; and Garrick's memory next,
When time has somewhat mellowed it, and made
The idol of our worship while he lived
The god of our idolatry once more,
Shall have its altar; and the world shall go
In pilgrimage to bow before his shrine.
The theatre, too small, shall suffocate
Its squeezed contents, and more than it admits

Shall sigh at their exclusion, and return
Ungratified. For there some noble lord
Shall stuff his shoulders with King Richard's bunch,
Or wrap himself in Hamlet's inky cloak,
And strut, and storm, and straddle, stamp, and stare,
To show the world how Garrick did not act,
For Garrick was a worshipper himself;
He drew the liturgy, and framed the rites
And solemn ceremonial of the day,
And called the world to worship on the banks
Of Avon famed in song. Ah! pleasant proof
That piety has still in human hearts
Some place, a spark or two not yet extinct.
The mulberry-tree was hung with blooming wreaths,
The mulberry-tree stood centre of the dance,
The mulberry-tree was hymned with dulcet airs,
And from his touchwood trunk the mulberry-tree
Supplied such relics as devotion holds
Still sacred, and preserves with pious care.
So 'twas a hallowed time: decorum reigned,
And mirth without offence. No few returned
Doubtless much edified, and all refreshed.
—Man praises man. The rabble all alive,
From tippling benches, cellars, stalls, and styes,
Swarm in the streets. The statesman of the day,
A pompous and slow-moving pageant, comes;
Some shout him, and some hang upon his car
To gaze in his eyes and bless him. Maidens wave
Their kerchiefs, and old women weep for joy
While others not so satisfied unhorse
The gilded equipage, and, turning loose
His steeds, usurp a place they well deserve.
Why? what has charmed them? Hath he saved the state?
No. Doth he purpose its salvation? No.
Enchanting novelty, that moon at full
That finds out every crevice of the head
That is not sound and perfect, hath in theirs
Wrought this disturbance. But the wane is near,
And his own cattle must suffice him soon.
Thus idly do we waste the breath of praise,
And dedicate a tribute, in its use
And just direction sacred, to a thing
Doomed to the dust, or lodged already there.

Encomium in old time was poet's work;
But, poets having lavishly long since
Exhausted all materials of the art,
The task now falls into the public hand;
And I, contented with a humble theme,
Have poured my stream of panegyric down
The vale of Nature, where it creeps and winds
Among her lovely works, with a secure
And unambitious course, reflecting clear
If not the virtues yet the worth of brutes.
And I am recompensed, and deem the toil
Of poetry not lost, if verse of mine
May stand between an animal and woe,
And teach one tyrant pity for his drudge.

The groans of Nature in this nether world,
Which Heaven has heard for ages, have an end.
Foretold by prophets, and by poets sung,
Whose fire was kindled at the prophets' lamp,
The time of rest, the promised Sabbath, comes.
Six thousand years of sorrow have well-nigh
Fulfilled their tardy and disastrous course
Over a sinful world; and what remains
Of this tempestuous state of human things,
Is merely as the working of a sea
Before a calm, that rocks itself to rest.
For He, whose car the winds are, and the clouds
The dust that waits upon His sultry march,
When sin hath moved Him, and His wrath is hot,
Shall visit earth in mercy; shall descend
Propitious, in His chariot paved with love,
And what His storms have blasted and defaced
For man's revolt, shall with a smile repair.

Sweet is the harp of prophecy; too sweet
Not to be wronged by a mere mortal touch;
Nor can the wonders it records be sung
To meaner music, and not suffer loss.
But when a poet, or when one like me,
Happy to rove among poetic flowers,
Though poor in skill to rear them, lights at last
On some fair theme, some theme divinely fair,
Such is the impulse and the spur he feels

To give it praise proportioned to its worth,
That not to attempt it, arduous as he deems
The labour, were a task more arduous still.

Oh scenes surpassing fable, and yet true,
Scenes of accomplished bliss! which who can see,
Though but in distant prospect, and not feel
His soul refreshed with foretaste of the joy?
Rivers of gladness water all the earth,
And clothe all climes with beauty; the reproach
Of barrenness is past. The fruitful field
Laughs with abundance, and the land once lean,
Or fertile only in its own disgrace,
Exults to see its thistly curse repealed.
The various seasons woven into one,
And that one season an eternal spring,
The garden fears no blight, and needs no fence,
For there is none to covet, all are full.
The lion and the libbard and the bear
Graze with the fearless flocks. All bask at noon
Together, or all gambol in the shade
Of the same grove, and drink one common stream.
Antipathies are none. No foe to man
Lurks in the serpent now. The mother sees,
And smiles to see, her infant's playful hand
Stretched forth to dally with the crested worm,
To stroke his azure neck, or to receive
The lambent homage of his arrowy tongue.
All creatures worship man, and all mankind
One Lord, one Father. Error has no place;
That creeping pestilence is driven away,
The breath of heaven has chased it. In the heart
No passion touches a discordant string,
But all is harmony and love. Disease
Is not. The pure and uncontaminated blood
Holds its due course, nor fears the frost of age.
One song employs all nations; and all cry,
"Worthy the Lamb, for He was slain for us!"
The dwellers in the vales and on the rocks
Shout to each other, and the mountain-tops
From distant mountains catch the flying joy,
Till nation after nation taught the strain,
Each rolls the rapturous Hosanna round.

121

Behold the measure of the promise filled,
See Salem built, the labour of a God!
Bright as a sun the sacred city shines;
All kingdoms and all princes of the earth
Flock to that light; the glory of all lands
Flows into her, unbounded is her joy
And endless her increase. Thy rams are there,
Nebaioth,* and the flocks of Kedar there;
The looms of Ormus, and the mines of Ind,
And Saba's spicy groves pay tribute there.
Praise is in all her gates. Upon her walls,
And in her streets, and in her spacious courts
Is heard salvation. Eastern Java there
Kneels with the native of the farthest West,
And AEthiopia spreads abroad the hand,
And worships. Her report has travelled forth
Into all lands. From every clime they come
To see thy beauty and to share thy joy,
O Sion! an assembly such as earth
Saw never; such as heaven stoops down to see.

* Nebaioth and Kedar, the sons of Ishmael, and progenitors of the Arabs, in the prophetic scripture here alluded to may be reasonably considered as representatives of the Gentiles at large. —C.

Thus heavenward all things tend. For all were once
Perfect, and all must be at length restored.
So God has greatly purposed; who would else
In His dishonoured works Himself endure
Dishonour, and be wronged without redress.
Haste then, and wheel away a shattered world,
Ye slow-revolving seasons! We would see
(A sight to which our eyes are strangers yet)
A world that does not dread and hate His laws,
And suffer for its crime: would learn how fair
The creature is that God pronounces good,
How pleasant in itself what pleases Him.
Here every drop of honey hides a sting;
Worms wind themselves into our sweetest flowers,
And even the joy, that haply some poor heart
Derives from heaven, pure as the fountain is,
Is sullied in the stream; taking a taint
From touch of human lips, at best impure.

Oh for a world in principle as chaste
As this is gross and selfish! over which
Custom and prejudice shall bear no sway,
That govern all things here, shouldering aside
The meek and modest Truth, and forcing her
To seek a refuge from the tongue of strife
In nooks obscure, far from the ways of men,
Where violence shall never lift the sword,
Nor cunning justify the proud man's wrong,
Leaving the poor no remedy but tears;
Where he that fills an office, shall esteem
The occasion it presents of doing good
More than the perquisite; where laws shall speak
Seldom, and never but as wisdom prompts,
And equity, not jealous more to guard
A worthless form, than to decide aright;
Where fashion shall not sanctify abuse,
Nor smooth good-breeding (supplemental grace)
With lean performance ape the work of love.

Come then, and added to Thy many crowns
Receive yet one, the crown of all the earth,
Thou who alone art worthy! it was Thine
By ancient covenant, ere nature's birth,
And Thou hast made it Thine by purchase since,
And overpaid its value with Thy blood.
Thy saints proclaim Thee King; and in their hearts
Thy title is engraven with a pen
Dipt in the fountain of eternal love.
Thy saints proclaim Thee King; and Thy delay
Gives courage to their foes, who, could they see
The dawn of Thy last advent, long-desired,
Would creep into the bowels of the hills,
And flee for safety to the falling rocks.
The very spirit of the world is tired
Of its own taunting question, asked so long,
"Where is the promise of your Lord's approach?"
The infidel has shot his bolts away,
Till, his exhausted quiver yielding none,
He gleans the blunted shafts that have recoiled,
And aims them at the shield of truth again.
The veil is rent, rent too by priestly hands,
That hides divinity from mortal eyes;

And all the mysteries to faith proposed,
Insulted and traduced, are cast aside,
As useless, to the moles and to the bats.
They now are deemed the faithful and are praised,
Who, constant only in rejecting Thee,
Deny Thy Godhead with a martyr's zeal,
And quit their office for their error's sake.
Blind and in love with darkness! yet even these
Worthy, compared with sycophants, who kneel,
Thy Name adoring, and then preach Thee man!
So fares Thy Church. But how Thy Church may fare,
The world takes little thought; who will may preach,
And what they will. All pastors are alike
To wandering sheep resolved to follow none.
Two gods divide them all, Pleasure and Gain;
For these they live, they sacrifice to these,
And in their service wage perpetual war
With conscience and with Thee. Lust in their hearts,
And mischief in their hands, they roam the earth
To prey upon each other; stubborn, fierce,
High-minded, foaming out their own disgrace.
Thy prophets speak of such; and noting down
The features of the last degenerate times,
Exhibit every lineament of these.
Come then, and added to Thy many crowns
Receive yet one as radiant as the rest,
Due to Thy last and most effectual work,
Thy Word fulfilled, the conquest of a world.

He is the happy man, whose life even now
Shows somewhat of that happier life to come;
Who, doomed to an obscure but tranquil state,
Is pleased with it, and, were he free to choose,
Would make his fate his choice; whom peace, the fruit
Of virtue, and whom virtue, fruit of faith,
Prepare for happiness; bespeak him one
Content indeed to sojourn while he must
Below the skies, but having there his home.
The world o'erlooks him in her busy search
Of objects more illustrious in her view;
And occupied as earnestly as she,
Though more sublimely, he o'erlooks the world.
She scorns his pleasures, for she knows them not;

He seeks not hers, for he has proved them vain.
He cannot skim the ground like summer birds
Pursuing gilded flies, and such he deems
Her honours, her emoluments, her joys;
Therefore in contemplation is his bliss,
Whose power is such, that whom she lifts from earth
She makes familiar with a heaven unseen,
And shows him glories yet to be revealed.
Not slothful he, though seeming unemployed,
And censured oft as useless. Stillest streams
Oft water fairest meadows; and the bird
That flutters least is longest on the wing.
Ask him, indeed, what trophies he has raised,
Or what achievements of immortal fame
He purposes, and he shall answer—None.
His warfare is within. There unfatigued
His fervent spirit labours. There he fights,
And there obtains fresh triumphs o'er himself,
And never-withering wreaths, compared with which
The laurels that a Caesar reaps are weeds.
Perhaps the self-approving haughty world,
That, as she sweeps him with her whistling silks,
Scarce deigns to notice him, or if she see,
Deems him a cipher in the works of God,
Receives advantage from his noiseless hours
Of which she little dreams. Perhaps she owes
Her sunshine and her rain, her blooming spring
And plenteous harvest, to the prayer he makes
When, Isaac-like, the solitary saint
Walks forth to meditate at eventide,
And think on her who thinks not for herself.
Forgive him then, thou bustler in concerns
Of little worth, and idler in the best,
If, author of no mischief and some good,
He seeks his proper happiness by means
That may advance, but cannot hinder thine.
Nor, though he tread the secret path of life,
Engage no notice, and enjoy much ease,
Account him an encumbrance on the state,
Receiving benefits, and rendering none.
His sphere though humble, if that humble sphere
Shine with his fair example, and though small
His influence, if that influence all be spent

In soothing sorrow and in quenching strife,
In aiding helpless indigence, in works
From which at least a grateful few derive
Some taste of comfort in a world of woe,
Then let the supercilious great confess
He serves his country; recompenses well
The state beneath the shadow of whose vine
He sits secure, and in the scale of life
Holds no ignoble, though a slighted place.
The man whose virtues are more felt than seen,
Must drop, indeed, the hope of public praise;
But he may boast, what few that win it can,
That if his country stand not by his skill,
At least his follies have not wrought her fall.
Polite refinement offers him in vain
Her golden tube, through which a sensual world
Draws gross impurity, and likes it well,
The neat conveyance hiding all the offence.
Not that he peevishly rejects a mode
Because that world adopts it. If it bear
The stamp and clear impression of good sense,
And be not costly more than of true worth,
He puts it on, and for decorum sake
Can wear it e'en as gracefully as she.
She judges of refinement by the eye,
He by the test of conscience, and a heart
Not soon deceived; aware that what is base
No polish can make sterling, and that vice,
Though well-perfumed and elegantly dressed,
Like an unburied carcass tricked with flowers,
Is but a garnished nuisance, fitter far
For cleanly riddance than for fair attire.
So life glides smoothly and by stealth away,
More golden than that age of fabled gold
Renowned in ancient song; not vexed with care,
Or stained with guilt, beneficent, approved
Of God and man, and peaceful in its end.

So glide my life away! and so at last,
My share of duties decently fulfilled,
May some disease, not tardy to perform
Its destined office, yet with gentle stroke,
Dismiss me weary to a safe retreat

Beneath the turf that I have often trod.
It shall not grieve me, then, that once, when called
To dress a Sofa with the flowers of verse,
I played awhile, obedient to the fair,
With that light task, but soon to please her more,
Whom flowers alone I knew would little please,
Let fall the unfinished wreath, and roved for fruit;
Roved far and gathered much; some harsh, 'tis true,
Picked from the thorns and briars of reproof,
But wholesome, well-digested; grateful some
To palates that can taste immortal truth;
Insipid else, and sure to be despised.
But all is in His hand whose praise I seek,
In vain the poet sings, and the world hears,
If He regard not, though divine the theme.
'Tis not in artful measures, in the chime
And idle tinkling of a minstrel's lyre,
To charm His ear, whose eye is on the heart;
Whose frown can disappoint the proudest strain,
Whose approbation—prosper even mine.

THE DIVERTING HISTORY OF JOHN GILPIN;

SHOWING HOW HE WENT FARTHER THAN HE INTENDED, AND CAME SAFE HOME AGAIN.

John Gilpin was a citizen
  Of credit and renown,
A train-band captain eke was he
  Of famous London town.

John Gilpin's spouse said to her dear,
  "Though wedded we have been
These twice ten tedious years, yet we
  No holiday have seen.

"To-morrow is our wedding-day,
  And we will then repair
Unto 'The Bell' at Edmonton,
  All in a chaise and pair.

"My sister and my sister's child,
  Myself and children three,
Will fill the chaise; so you must ride
  On horseback after we."

He soon replied, "I do admire
  Of womankind but one,
And you are she, my dearest dear,
  Therefore it shall be done.

"I am a linen-draper bold,
  As all the world doth know,
And my good friend the Calender
  Will lend his horse to go."

Quoth Mistress Gilpin, "That's well said;
  And, for that wine is dear,
We will be furnished with our own,
  Which is both bright and clear."

John Gilpin kissed his loving wife;
  O'erjoyed was he to find

That though on pleasure she was bent,
  She had a frugal mind.

The morning came, the chaise was brought,
  But yet was not allowed
To drive up to the door, lest all
  Should say that she was proud.

So three doors off the chaise was stayed,
  Where they did all get in;
Six precious souls, and all agog
  To dash through thick and thin.

Smack went the whip, round went the wheels,
  Were never folk so glad;
The stones did rattle underneath
  As if Cheapside were mad.

John Gilpin at his horse's side
  Seized fast the flowing mane,
And up he got, in haste to ride,
  But soon came down again;

For saddle-tree scarce reached had he,
  His journey to begin,
When, turning round his head, he saw
  Three customers come in.

So down he came; for loss of time,
  Although it grieved him sore,
Yet loss of pence, full well he knew,
  Would trouble him much more.

'Twas long before the customers
  Were suited to their mind.
When Betty, screaming, came down stairs,
  "The wine is left behind!"

"Good lack!" quoth he; "yet bring it me,
  My leathern belt likewise,
In which I bear my trusty sword,
  When I do exercise."

Now Mistress Gilpin (careful soul!)
　Had two stone bottles found,
To hold the liquor that she loved,
　And keep it safe and sound.

Each bottle had a curling ear,
　Through which the belt he drew,
And hung a bottle on each side,
　To make his balance true.

Then over all, that he might be
　Equipped from top to toe,
His long red cloak, well brushed and neat,
　He manfully did throw.

Now see him mounted once again
　Upon his nimble steed,
Full slowly pacing o'er the stones
　With caution and good heed!

But, finding soon a smoother road
　Beneath his well-shod feet,
The snorting beast began to trot,
　Which galled him in his seat.

So, "Fair and softly," John he cried,
　But John he cried in vain;
That trot became a gallop soon,
　In spite of curb and rein.

So stooping down, as needs he must
　Who cannot sit upright,
He grasped the mane with both his hands,
　And eke with all his might.

His horse, who never in that sort
　Had handled been before,
What thing upon his back had got
　Did wonder more and more.

Away went Gilpin, neck or naught;
　Away went hat and wig;
He little dreamt, when he set out,

Of running such a rig.

The wind did blow, the cloak did fly,
  Like streamer long and gay,
Till, loop and button failing both,
  At last it flew away.

Then might all people well discern
  The bottles he had slung;
A bottle swinging at each side,
  As hath been said or sung.

The dogs did bark, the children screamed,
  Up flew the windows all;
And every soul cried out, "Well done!"
  As loud as he could bawl.

Away went Gilpin—who but he?
  His fame soon spread around—
He carries weight! he rides a race!
  'Tis for a thousand pound!

And still, as fast as he drew near,
  'Twas wonderful to view
How in a trice the turnpike men
  Their gates wide open threw.

And now, as he went bowing down
  His reeking head full low,
The bottles twain behind his back
  Were shattered at a blow.

Down ran the wine into the road,
  Most piteous to be seen,
Which made his horse's flanks to smoke
  As they had basted been.

But still he seemed to carry weight,
  With leathern girdle braced;
For all might see the bottle-necks
  Still dangling at his waist.

Thus all through merry Islington

These gambols he did play,
And till he came unto the Wash
  Of Edmonton so gay.

And there he threw the wash about
  On both sides of the way,
Just like unto a trundling mop,
  Or a wild goose at play.

At Edmonton, his loving wife
  From the bal-cony spied
Her tender husband, wondering much
  To see how he did ride.

"Stop, stop, John Gilpin!—here's the house!"
  They all at once did cry;
"The dinner waits, and we are tired."
  Said Gilpin, "So am I!"

But yet his horse was not a whit
  Inclined to tarry there;
For why?—his owner had a house
  Full ten miles off, at Ware.

So like an arrow swift he flew,
  Shot by an archer strong;
So did he fly—which brings me to
  The middle of my song.

Away went Gilpin, out of breath,
  And sore against his will,
Till at his friend the Calender's
  His horse at last stood still.

The Calender, amazed to see
  His neighbour in such trim,
Laid down his pipe, flew to the gate,
  And thus accosted him:—

"What news? what news? your tidings tell:
  Tell me you must and shall—
Say why bareheaded you are come,
  Or why you come at all."

Now Gilpin had a pleasant wit,
  And loved a timely joke;
And thus unto the Calender
  In merry guise he spoke:

"I came because your horse would come;
  And if I well forebode,
My hat and wig will soon be here;
  They are upon the road."

The Calender, right glad to find
  His friend in merry pin,
Returned him not a single word,
  But to the house went in;

Whence straight he came with hat and wig,
  A wig that flowed behind,
A hat not much the worse for wear,
  Each comely in its kind.

He held them up, and, in his turn,
  Thus showed his ready wit, —
"My head is twice as big as yours;
  They therefore needs must fit.

"But let me scrape the dirt away
  That hangs upon your face;
And stop and eat, for well you may
  Be in a hungry case."

Says John, "It is my wedding-day,
  And all the world would stare,
If wife should dine at Edmonton,
  And I should dine at Ware."

So turning to his horse, he said,
  "I am in haste to dine;
'Twas for your pleasure you came here,
  You shall go back for mine."

Ah, luckless speech, and bootless boast!
  For which he paid full dear;
For while he spake, a braying ass

Did sing most loud and clear;

Whereat his horse did snort as he
  Had heard a lion roar,
And galloped off with all his might,
  As he had done before.

Away went Gilpin, and away
  Went Gilpin's hat and wig;
He lost them sooner than at first,
  For why?—they were too big.

Now Mistress Gilpin, when she saw
  Her husband posting down
Into the country far away,
  She pulled out half-a-crown.

And thus unto the youth she said,
  That drove them to "The Bell,"
"This shall be yours when you bring back
  My husband safe and well."

The youth did ride, and soon did meet
  John coming back amain,
Whom in a trice he tried to stop
  By catching at his rein;

But not performing what he meant,
  And gladly would have done,
The frighted steed he frighted more,
  And made him faster run.

Away went Gilpin, and away
  Went postboy at his heels,
The postboy's horse right glad to miss
  The lumbering of the wheels.

Six gentlemen upon the road
  Thus seeing Gilpin fly,
With postboy scampering in the rear,
  They raised the hue and cry:

"Stop thief! stop thief!—a highwayman!"

Not one of them was mute;
And all and each that passed that way
  Did join in the pursuit.

And now the turnpike gates again
  Flew open in short space,
The tollmen thinking, as before,
  That Gilpin rode a race.

And so he did, and won it too,
  For he got first to town;
Nor stopped till where he had got up
  He did again get down.

Now let us sing, "Long live the king,
  And Gilpin, long live he;
And when he next doth ride abroad,
  May I be there to see!"

AN EPISTLE TO JOSEPH HILL, ESQ.

DEAR JOSEPH,—five and twenty years ago—
Alas, how time escapes!—'tis even so—
With frequent intercourse, and always sweet
And always friendly, we were wont to cheat
A tedious hour—and now we never meet.
As some grave gentleman in Terence says
('Twas therefore much the same in ancient days),
"Good lack, we know not what to-morrow brings—
Strange fluctuation of all human things!"
True. Changes will befall, and friends may part,
But distance only cannot change the heart:
And were I called to prove the assertion true,
One proof should serve—a reference to you.

Whence comes it, then, that in the wane of life,
Though nothing have occurred to kindle strife,
We find the friends we fancied we had won,
Though numerous once, reduced to few or none?
Can gold grow worthless that has stood the touch?
No. Gold they seemed, but they were never such.
Horatio's servant once, with bow and cringe,
Swinging the parlour-door upon its hinge,
Dreading a negative, and overawed
Lest he should trespass, begged to go abroad.
"Go, fellow!—whither?"—turning short about—
"Nay. Stay at home; you're always going out."—
"'Tis but a step, sir; just at the street's end."
"For what?"—"An please you, sir, to see a friend."
"A friend!" Horatio cried, and seemed to start;
"Yea, marry shalt thou, and with all my heart—
And fetch my cloak, for though the night be raw
I'll see him too—the first I ever saw."

I knew the man, and knew his nature mild,
And was his plaything often when a child;
But somewhat at that moment pinched him close,
Else he was seldom bitter or morose.
Perhaps, his confidence just then betrayed,
His grief might prompt him with the speech he made;
Perhaps 'twas mere good-humour gave it birth,

The harmless play of pleasantry and mirth.
Howe'er it was, his language in my mind
Bespoke at least a man that knew mankind.

But not to moralise too much, and strain
To prove an evil of which all complain
(I hate long arguments, verbosely spun),
One story more, dear Hill, and I have done.
Once on a time, an emperor, a wise man.
No matter where, in China or Japan,
Decreed that whosoever should offend
Against the well-known duties of a friend,
Convicted once, should ever after wear
But half a coat, and show his bosom bare;
The punishment importing this, no doubt,
That all was naught within and all found out.

Oh happy Britain! we have not to fear
Such hard and arbitrary measure here;
Else could a law, like that which I relate,
Once have the sanction of our triple state,
Some few that I have known in days of old
Would run most dreadful risk of catching cold.
While you, my friend, whatever wind should blow,
Might traverse England safely to and fro,
An honest man, close buttoned to the chin,
Broad-cloth without, and a warm heart within.

TO MARY.

The twentieth year is well-nigh past
Since first our sky was overcast,
Ah, would that this might be the last!
　　My Mary!

Thy spirits have a fainter flow,
I see thee daily weaker grow—
'Twas my distress that brought thee low,
　　My Mary!

Thy needles, once a shining store,
For my sake restless heretofore,
Now rust disused, and shine no more,
　　My Mary!

For though thou gladly wouldst fulfil
The same kind office for me still,
Thy sight now seconds not thy will,
　　My Mary!

But well thou playedst the housewife's part,
And all thy threads with magic art
Have wound themselves about this heart,
　　My Mary!

Thy indistinct expressions seem
Like language uttered in a dream;
Yet me they charm, whate'er the theme,
　　My Mary!

Thy silver locks, once auburn bright,
Are still more lovely in my sight
Than golden beams of orient light,
　　My Mary!

For could I view nor them nor thee,
What sight worth seeing could I see?
The sun would rise in vain for me,
　　My Mary!

Partakers of thy sad decline,
Thy hands their little force resign;
Yet gently prest, press gently mine,
  My Mary!

Such feebleness of limbs thou prov'st,
That now at every step thou mov'st
Upheld by two, yet still thou lov'st,
  My Mary!

And still to love, though prest with ill,
In wintry age to feel no chill,
With me, is to be lovely still,
  My Mary!

But ah! by constant heed I know,
How oft the sadness that I show,
Transforms thy smiles to looks of woe,
  My Mary!

And should my future lot be cast
With much resemblance of the past,
Thy worn-out heart will break at last,
  My Mary!

8483303R00083

Printed in Great Britain
by Amazon.co.uk, Ltd.,
Marston Gate.